THE MULTICULTURAL CHALLENGE

THE MULTICULTURAL CHALLENGE
A Visual-Cultural Guide to Coping in the Global Era

Ingrid Aall

South Asian Studies Association
www.sasia.or

Printed in the United States of America
Frist Edition

ISBN 978-0-9834472-0-7 (paperback)

South Asian Studies Association
a public benefit, non-profit corporation, EID 26-1437834
www.sasia.org

To my father, the philosopher, Dr. Anathon Fredric August Aall. His legacy of dreaming and acting in harmony with his vision is my heritage.

CONTENTS

Part II Cultural Literacy

FOREWORD

The 34,000 students at California State University, Long Beach represent a microcosmic, multicultural mirror of our world. The students and faculty, coming from all over the world, bring a wealth of knowledge, diversity, and global awareness to our campus. As one of the nation's most diverse and largest universities, we constantly strive to be ever more globally engaged. Furthermore, we firmly believe that it is a necessity to provide our students with an international perspective through educational experiences and opportunities. In preparing our students for these opportunities, curricula and text books that further this goal are highly valued and bring fresh perspectives to new and old fields of study. In this context, *The Multicultural Challenge: A Visual-Cultural Guide to Coping in the Global Era*, by Dr. Ingrid Aall, emerita faculty member of Art History, is such a resource.

This book is designed to prepare our students for the interactive and increasingly engaged global society. The text clearly defines concepts that are central to numerous contemporary issues, all of which explain the difficulties arising from encounters with the unfamiliar. The book acknowledges and addresses many central problems facing current students as they navigate through rapidly changing environments that may be familiar to some and very unfamiliar to others. Key concepts introduced and defined include culture shock, future shock, cultural relativity; examples demonstrate how students can expand their visual perceptual sensations without singling out a particular culture. As an introductory guide, this resource alternates between similarities and differences of known and lesser-known cultures, seen from the perspectives of the student.

A central theme throughout the text, but particularly in the latter chapters, is the role that art plays as a mirror for our society. Utilizing art as a means to understand transformative cultures will increasingly become a vital tool for not only students but others throughout society. In fact, the constant flux of art has become increasingly similar to the constantly changing environmental circumstances shaping our evolving societies.

Furthermore, the appendices provide a series of exercises and experiments that help students understand the material being presented and, at the same time, challenge them to conduct self-evaluation. These exercises seek a personal reaction, a personal response from the student, and then provide an opportunity to place these responses in a broad framework of art and culture.

Using visual literacy as a guide, the book covers a variety of issues. In the chapters, issues such as immigration, the impact of modern technology, and the impact of postmodern art on contemporary ethics are explored and evaluated. Throughout the book, students are challenged to take a personal journey in visual and cultural literacy and to reflect on the shared responsibility of the future of our world. I encourage you to accept Dr. Ingrid Aall's challenge.

F. King Alexander
President, California State University Long Beach

PREFACE

From cradle to grave, we're continuously expanding our consciousness in terms of our interior space and the outside world. We move from the center within ourselves to larger and larger spaces, connecting physical and mental horizons: from a mother's womb to family, village, region, state, nation, continent, and world, creating ever-widening circles of understanding. Yet we remain aware of our starting point. The journey is spatial on the one hand and spiritual on the other, the two merging as our conscious reality.

Global consciousness develops in a process not unlike that of the formation of coral reefs. Coral is a living organism that proliferates in the ocean's waters, sometimes connecting to other coral masses. Such links become strong and foster many life forms. The complex structure of the reef is similar to the global community, in that it houses a vast diversity of species, yet functions to the benefit of all. Just as these species cohabit the reef, we humans, in all our diversity, cohabit our globe.

This book explores the many hurdles we face, starting off as mono-cultural people operating from within a local or provincial frame of reference, and becoming open-minded people unencumbered by preconceptions, discrimination, and prejudice, identifying with and appreciating cultural diversity.

As our point of departure, we'll address art as the means to understand the culture from which it originates, and culture as the means for understanding art, each inspiring the other. Anthropologist Claude Lévi-Strauss argues that we can find parallel homologies in institutions of any given culture at any given time that reflect and illuminate one another. When we see how things stand in relation to each other, a pattern emerges. Once we see this pattern, we understand our interconnectedness and develop the ability to knowingly cope with what we see. Visual and cultural literacy means being able to recognize the paradox of this perfect catch-22 paradigm. Visual perception doesn't occur in an emotional and intellectual vacuum, but is influenced by mental attitudes and habits. These in turn are shaped by cultural and educational experiences, as well as our cumulative contact with art. A major obstacle in achieving cultural literacy lies in preconscious mental habits ingrained from our childhood. Mental habits include all of our assumptions and presuppositions—everything we take for granted. We all have these; they color our interactions with our fellow human beings, and hinder our ability to remain objective.

For the purposes of this book, rather than using the quantitative research approach, which requires verifiable documentation through statistical data, I'll apply my own interpretation of the qualitative method, which validates emotions as a primary interpretive component in using art as the training ground for practicing visual aptitude. We'll then graduate to the big picture: using art as the subtext for understanding people and their culture, thus preparing ourselves for our future in the global community.

As a qualitative researcher I am a *bricoleur,* employing a variety of methodologies and common sense to arrive at answers to questions raised in the following contexts:

- personal experiences and notes from field studies in numerous Western and Eastern countries
- comments from students of all ages, genders, and cultures who've participated in the Cross-Cultural Visual Literacy course that I developed and taught over a decade at California State University Long Beach
- Countless hours researching a wide variety of publications and relevant Internet sites.

The reader will notice extensive examples from China throughout the text. This shouldn't be read as any particular cultural bias on my part; rather, as the fastest growing nation both in terms of population and economics, China presents an excellent example of the patterns of cultural shifts that all 21st-century nations face to some degree.

Throughout the five chapters of this book, awareness and creativity are key to the recurring themes of education, knowledge, self-awareness, and personal responsibility—the pillars that will support our ongoing construction of a sustainable, global human reef.

The appendices include a number of experiments and exercises designed for readers wishing to monitor their progress through self-assessment. Those wishing to further their studies will find relevant references in the bibliography. Counterintuitive as it may seem for a study of visual literacy, I've included no illustrations, as the text is meant to challenge readers to draw on their own resourcefulness in using the myriad images readily available on the Internet, in traditional print, and at museums and galleries. By focusing on self-selected visuals, we can monitor our perceptions as we reaffirm the concept of the world itself as our canvas.

The key that opens the door to global citizenship is the validation of the strength inherent in our interdependence. The importance of both the Internet and the computer as facilitators and equalizers in this process is germane to our discussion.

The aim of this book is to help readers see the illusory nature of our conscious realities, an obligatory competency for anyone aspiring to become a global citizen operating from within changing perspectives. Given the onslaught of unrelenting new technological developments, as well as unforeseeable environmental changes, the future requires us to question the familiar and adapt new lifestyles while unlearning old ones.

This book is presented in two parts.

In Part I, Visual Literacy, we study the aspects of art that give us pleasure and insight into creativity in the art-making process; namely, we explore how art

- communicates ideas and concepts
- stimulates emotional responses
- challenges our visual aptitude and imagination
- makes us see reality from a perspective broader than our own
- inspires introspective contemplation
- reminds us of realties behind and beyond optical appearance
- becomes what we make of it, be it beautiful or provocative
- operates within a context
- changes its meaning as context changes in respect to time and place

- engages the heart and mind to create visual manifestations
- signifies culture and transmits culture-specific values.

Chapter 1, Processing Visual Perceptions, addresses visual literacy from the perspective of an active viewer. The chapter identifies and explores the variety of ways we see and perceive visual statements. Through examples and practical techniques we'll learn how to monitor, control, and expand our visual experiences.

Chapter 2, Decoding Art, focuses on art not just for art's sake, but also because art is, I believe, the most fecund expression of culture. Art serves as a reliable platform for our initial understanding of the culture from which it originated. First, we'll address the visual aspects of a work of art, and how to analyze and enjoy them. We'll consider the art-making process, while challenging ourselves as viewers to apply our new ways of seeing. As we study technical aspects as well as cultural context, we'll become aware of the potentials and limitations of the medium in which the art object is executed.

Since art is never created in a vacuum, we'll define its cultural context and the degree to which the work relates to its culture. Just as artists apply their creative energy in the process of producing art, we as viewers must also use our creativity in the process of perceiving art. Then we'll discuss the similarities of the process of decoding art to those of decoding people and cultures.

Chapter 3, Decoding People, applies the method of decoding art to viewing and understanding people. The idea is that people are the products of their own creativity, and can therefore be studied and analyzed as art. When we want to know a person, we approach that person with many questions in mind. Body language, attire, age, gender, and general appearance give us visual clues that, together with additional information, place the person in a socio-cultural context. Based on this context, we form a preliminary impression. Over time, if we're capable of considering, reconsidering, and modifying our first impressions, we can learn to accept one another's perceived imperfections, be they physical or mental. As we practice this empathetic mode of seeing, we see that people play a variety of roles; they look and act according to given situations and cultural contexts.

In Part II, Cultural Literacy, we'll examine culture more closely, building on its interconnections with art:

- Art has historically served to educate preliterate people, and still does.
- Art does not appear in a vacuum, but is a manifestation of culture.
- Art is the collective dream of a people, defining culture.
- Art expresses latent messages in advance of their subsequent social and cultural expressions.
- Culture, like art, is expressed and experienced both individually and collectively.
- Each culture expresses both culture-specific and common characteristics.
- A culture doesn't exist in isolation, but intersects with other cultures, lending expression and meaning to multiculturalism.
- Multiculturalism spans globally, redefining the traditional meaning of singular cultures.
- The cultural paradigm shift stresses individual responsibility and active participation in the creative process of an emerging global culture.
- Our ultimate challenge: creatively meeting today's challenges and transcending prior limitations in preparation for membership in tomorrow's fully integrated, multicultural, global community.

In chapter 4, Processing and Decoding Cultures, we view culture as a process, moving from our individual perspective in our inherited culture to experience that of an adopted culture. We'll take an immigrant's point of view and explore the various phases of cultural acclimatization an *outsider* undergoes in the quest to become an *insider*. Those of us who've already traveled abroad can identify with the immigrant experience, as we too have felt, albeit to a lesser degree, the discomfort of culture shock or the isolation and vulnerability of negotiating unfamiliar situations. These of course are challenges that everyone will eventually have to face in adjusting to the dynamics, riches, and perils of living in a multicultural society.

Chapter 5, Understanding Our Present and Creating Our Future, disengages from the focus on the individual and addresses the collective. We'll examine the impact that technological advances in electronic communications have had on our awareness of the world as an interconnected entity. We'll discus access to the Internet as an equalizer and its function in facilitating a democratization of knowledge that, until recently, had remained in the hands of a privileged few.

Using the same methods that we applied in Chapter 3 to decode other cultural expressions, we'll investigate characteristics of Postmodernism and popular culture in their many visual manifestations. What can postmodern art tell us about the nature of our current culture, and how does it foreshadow future trends?

Finally, we'll use our findings to index the challenges that interconnecting cultures must acknowledge and resolve. The book concludes with a discussion of our collective responsibility in shaping the content of cultural globalization. Taking responsibility means involving ourselves, not merely as observers, but as participants.

Our hearts and eyes are the shortest road to our perception of reality. We are not responsible for what we feel; feelings are not, in and of themselves, moral or immoral, but we are responsible for what we do with our feelings and how we react to them. No matter how weak or strong our feelings may be, we should listen to them. Feelings left unexamined can fester, inhibiting our ability to adapt to our circumstances. We must try to understand their origins. The hope is that as we become aware of our feelings, they'll develop into constructive thoughts. Anxiety of the unknown disseminates when we understand how our lives unfold in the cultural, social, and political contexts of our times.

ACKNOWLEDGMENTS

To my innumerable old and new friends, scholars, students, and travelers I have encountered through the years both at home and abroad, I am tremendously grateful. For ideas and thoughts you have offered, I thank each and every one of you.

Among the many outstanding teachers at the University of Chicago, especially memorable were the late humanist, Edward Dimock, my thesis advisor, and the late Mircea Eliade, the immigrant scholar, artist, and teacher. I continue to be inspired by their generosity of mind.

At the embryonic stages of this book, the late August Coppola, renowned educator, author, and friend, was a major influence. While working together on his interdisciplinary project, "Explorations in Cultural Creativity," he forced me to see more than was visible, opening my eyes to multiple ways of seeing.

To my friend, Emmy Award winner and best selling author Camryn Manheim, I owe special thanks. After a minute with the earliest version of the manuscript, she pushed it away and candidly stated, "Unreadable." This made me rethink the entire project that led to countless rewrites.

My older sister, Professor Emerita of the University of British Columbia, Dr. Louise Jilek-Aall, a psychiatrist and cultural anthropologist, has always shown interest in my endeavors. She patiently read and criticized several of the earliest drafts.

I would like to acknowledge the role California State University, Long Beach played in providing encouragement, grants, and sabbatical leaves. I salute the Art Department for allowing me, together with my ethnically diverse students, the freedom to explore topics ranging from the dynamics of race to immigration in an atmosphere of mutual trust and respect. In this environment, students willingly shared the complexities of their personal and multicultural experiences.

I am further indebted to colleagues and friends for standing by me through the many years it took to process the material, and for their relentless criticism, both positive and negative. Among them were artists, fiercely committed to their own arguments, Liu Go Sung, Frances Valesco, the late Kanwal Krishna, and Josef Herman. Though their arguments were valuable, I take full responsibility for the opinions expressed in this book. These are solely my own.

Without the contributions of my editor, Dean Huffaker, who brought helpful suggestions and order to my manuscript, this book would not have been completed. Dean, I appreciate your sensitivity and grasp of the material.

Untold hours of discussions with Liv Elin Haugland clarified many problems shared by immigrants, and her literary competence also contributed to the final draft. A very special thanks goes to my friend, world famous book designer Tini Miura, for her artistic interpretation gracing the cover of my book.

Finally, my heartfelt appreciation goes to the students, my curious and adventurous fellow travelers in our multicultural world.

PART I
VISUAL LITERACY

1

Processing Visual Perceptions

We often refer to eyes as our *windows to the world,* or *windows to the soul.* The English language uses a vast array of terms and phrases to describe how we perceive, such as *gawking, watching intently, gazing in amazement, staring like a deer caught in the headlights,* and so on. People can be *farsighted, shortsighted, sharp-sighted,* or *dim-sighted.* Each of these terms has either a positive or negative connotation—rarely does a term describing visual perception convey neutrality.

Vision provides us with rich sensory information—even the way a person glances at you tells you something about that person. Writers, in bringing their characters to life, use descriptive terms relating to the connection between sight and emotions, and thus give us tools to interpret the attitude behind the viewer's physical act of seeing. Accordingly, staring eyes signify an unsophisticated or scared person; downcast eyes, a modest person; wet eyes, an emotional person; shifting eyes, a liar.

A culture's language reveals what is central to that culture. Consider the primacy of visual language over spoken and written language, illustrated by the vast cross-cultural vocabulary of images. For example, if you want to communicate "butterfly," simply present an actual butterfly or its visual image, and it's immediately and universally apprehended as a butterfly. On the other hand, if you want to communicate "butterfly" verbally across cultures, you have to contend with a different language for each culture. The English word *butterfly* is not as easily recognized by non-English speakers: in Spanish it is *mariposa*; in French, *papillon*; in German, *Schmetterling;* in Swedish, *fjæril;* in Japanese, *chodo*; each language has its own designation for the same object. Obviously, no matter how hard you try, these various verbal utterances, in and of themselves, offer no clue as to their meaning. In the life of an infant, the child can respond to visual stimuli long before being able to interpret verbal communications.

Coping with different words for *butterfly* seldom has serious sociopolitical ramifications, but communication breakdowns in technological, medical, or business contexts can be disastrous. In order to ensure that all customers understand their electricity bills, big utilities like Southern California Edison print bills not only in English, but also in Spanish, Khmer, and Vietnamese, reflecting the economic realities of our multicultural world.

Usually when we listen to a person speak, our eyes independently form an opinion about the speaker. If we observe dissonance between appearance and speech, we instinctively accept what we see over what we hear. As the saying goes, "seeing is believing." What we don't realize is that, while we do believe what we see, the danger lies in the fact that we also have a tendency to see what we believe. To graduate beyond the amateur viewer status, we must become aware of the complexity of visual perception in order to understand the extent to which perceptions are influenced by our attitudes and previous experiences.

The starting point and basis of our study is to become aware of our eyes as agents of information. When we train our eyes to see beyond our preconceptions, our visual perception becomes more trustworthy, moving toward the goal expressed in the saying, "seeing is knowing." To assume that the way we perceive reality is universal, however, is a notion certainly worthy of unlearning. As our perceptual competency matures, we realize that perceptions vary according to the viewer's attitude, experiences, and expectations. Depending on the viewer, responses to visual stimuli range from pure gut-level, subconscious, emotive reactions, to the intellectual and rational. In fact, an individual's reactions to various visual stimuli, including art, are governed by the individual's particular cultural heritage, education, and level of awareness. Awareness of perception as a layered process is crucial to enabling control over perceptions. However, perceptions and responses depend on mental as well as physical factors caused by stress, pain, or medication, all circumstances over which the viewer may have little control. A viewer's moods allow the same visual statement to appear different at different times.

The fact that we see what we're predisposed to see is a universal phenomenon. I've dramatized this tendency in the classroom through the following activity: Introducing the activity as an exercise in visual perception, I'd ask my students to observe and describe a photograph. The photograph illustrated a medical article discussing the harm done to children by pregnant mothers ingesting thalidomide (a medicine previously thought to relieve morning sickness). Timid-looking children, dressed in scanty underwear, standing barefoot, facing the photographer, could be clearly observed. When asked what they saw, students independently reported on the number of males and females in the picture, and on the fact that the children's clothing seemed soiled and somewhat tattered. None of the students registered that each child lacked one or both arms. How did the students miss such significant details? We had previously discussed the relationship between poverty and clothing types, as well as other visual manifestations of indigence. Therefore, the students' attention focused on aspects related to that discussion. Unaware of the context in which the photograph was taken, the students weren't looking for birth defects, demonstrating that, as amateur viewers, we often miss what we don't expect to see.

Young children, on the other hand, see with their hearts as well as their minds. They approach the world with their total being, in a naive way and without stereotypical expectations. Some adults retain this childlike way of seeing, to a degree, reflecting an overwhelming emotional frame of reference. After practicing the range of perceptual modes discussed in this chapter, you too will find your way of seeing permanently altered, providing an escape from the perceptual habits that years of living have produced.

Artists, cognizant of the subjective quality of perception, are constantly researching, aspiring to transcend traditionally accepted limitations in order to goad the public into discovering new ways of seeing. Impressionism (also known as optical mixing) and Op art (optical art) are a few examples of art movements of the last few centuries that illustrate the results of such inquiries.[1] Modern artists in particular expose and challenge the public with their unique paintings, highlighting the relative nature of our subjective perceptions of reality. If this sounds like circular reasoning, there's a good reason for it: seeing is interpreting—a layered process that sometimes requires a reconditioning of unconsciously acquired visual and mental habits. In this way of thinking about seeing, what is seen is not about what there is to be observed, but who is doing the seeing. No object, no art, appears in a vacuum. Interpreting a visual statement means taking its context into consideration. The passive viewer merely *reacts* to visual statements; the informed viewer *responds*. The active viewer appreciates the difference between reacting and responding. The more aware you become of the perceptual process, the more you'll see.

Becoming an Active Viewer

Visual perception, for those fortunate enough to have unimpaired vision, would seem to be an activity as natural as breathing. But to comprehend the full scope of our visual perception, we must first become conscious of its process. Once the perceptual process becomes a conscious one, the viewer can elect to trade in old, habitual practices for newer, enriching ones.

The classic example of the half-empty/half-full glass demonstrates how a visual perception can be interpreted: what we see depends on our awareness and attitude. Since we can only see as far as our own perceptual horizon, a self-sustained appreciation of culture-specific perspectives best begins with a clear comprehension of our own, person-specific vantage point. In other words, in order to extract the most from a visual statement, we need to sensitize ourselves to our visual environment and become aware of the role we ourselves play in the process.

Perceptual aptitude and attitude are relative to individual education and experiences. To experience optimal perceptual awareness, we must learn to look beyond our initial emotional response, and engage in rational, intellectual, conceptual inquiry. Such inquiry calls on every mode of seeing available to us, particularly when we study works of art. Our ultimate goal of visual literacy is to master every aspect of our visual process, the sensory as well as the conceptual. Training ourselves to consciously and creatively combine the various modes of perception that we possess can free us of our preconditioned patterns of seeing.

Experiencing what happens when we're blindfolded and have to negotiate in darkness can help us gain a new perspective on the visual capacity that we often take for granted. Try the "Deprivation of Sight" experiment in appendix A on page 126—it should dramatize both the degree to which you rely on passive viewing and the access you have to additional perceptual modes that are instrumental to active viewing. After this experience, one of my students made the following observation:

It feels weird—like there is nothing else around me but space—kind of like floating in air. I was thinking that I could hear myself think; my thoughts seemed very loud in my head. I suppose perception is not only what you see, but also how you think and feel about what is around you.

What modes of perception do we possess and use in varying degrees on a daily basis? The table below identifies three distinct categories of visual perception—subjective, objective, and integrative. Their order in the table reflects a natural sequence of the perceptual process, although the sequence of the modes within each category doesn't necessarily indicate a hierarchy of importance.

Modes of Seeing

Subjective

- Spatial orientation
- Recognition of form
- Association and expectation
- Contemplation
- Empathy

Objective

- Observation and description
- Analysis

Integrative

- Ordinary and creative meditation
- Discovery
- Interpretation and assessment

The remainder of this chapter presents these modes of visual perception in more detail. The more you practice using each mode, the more readily available each will be to you. Eventually, your skill in negotiating these modes will enhance your appreciation of any visual statement, be it a face, the person it belongs to, or that person's culture. You'll also discover the difference between responding actively and reacting passively to a visual statement.

Seeing Subjectively

The only reality there is, is a do-it-yourself amalgamation of our perceptions of it. Reality is the projection of our subjective perception that we use to define it for ourselves—and others, since, as the expression goes, "there's safety in numbers." Our aim is to broaden our visual experiences, and while we're at it, to remember our most intimate and personal ways of experiencing what we see. The subjective modes include several ways of engaging perception. According to mood, interest, and awareness, each of us approaches a viewing target differently. In bringing subjective perception to a level of consciousness, we note five identifiable, subjective perceptual pathways that normally are activated at the beginning of a viewing experience: spatial orientation, recognition of form, association and expectation, contemplation, and empathy. The main characteristics of these modes relate to perceptions that are not dominated by reason alone, but in equal or greater degree, are derived from internal emotional layers.

Here our private culture-conditioned views come into play independent of conscious monitoring. Allowing time for unselfconscious perception is like stopping to listen to our hearts. This is the precondition for examining and practicing the subjective modes. If we are to advance beyond the primary reaction of like or dislike, if we are to learn to accept and embrace things that are foreign to our way of thinking, we must probe the cause of our responses and search for the origins of our likes, dislikes, or plain rejection, as the case may be.

Spatial Orientation

Among the modes of visual perception, orientation constitutes the initial stage. Simply stated, orientation configures spatial relationships. It's an unconscious process in which we assign meaning to visual data. Orientation establishes a relationship between the viewer's physical position relative to the position of objects, a relationship we spontaneously engage in every time we look at something. We've seen what a dog does when entering a room—it sniffs while turning round and round before settling to lie down, usually facing the direction of the door.

Driving a vehicle incorporates some aspects of discerning spatial relations that we take for granted. A driver's visual experience varies with the speed. When driving slowly, we're able to perceive details. But as the car speeds up, we only capture small snapshots of everything as our eyes move from spot to spot, and although objects have changed in size since the last time we looked at them, we still sense the continuity of images. Distant objects appear almost as if standing still. Our sense of movement, like all our senses, is relative to changing situations. Driving means moving, which in turn implies an intensified need for spatial orientation. Typically the driver and the passenger will notice different things.

While, initially, scanning is useful because it gives you a quick overview of the surrounding spaces, scanning alone is a limiting mode of perception because it doesn't register details. In our fast-paced society, people who become accustomed to scanning find that their ability to engage in sustained focus on one motionless object has deteriorated.

TV similarly encourages a scanning habit that over time easily becomes a habitual way of perception. For orientation purposes, scanning makes sense, but to gain more detailed information, focused concentration needs to be cultivated with conscious and deliberate effort.

These concepts relating to vision are also true for our perceptions of society as a whole. When we meet people, visit new places, participate in business meetings, or have an argument, we may be stuck in the habit of applying only the superficial orientation mode. Although this mode feels adequate for assessing basic circumstances, on deeper reflection we may realize that we've overlooked something essential.

Recognition of Form

Imagine you're waking up heavily drugged after an operation. You're aware of lights and sounds out there, all of which seem disconnected. Voices are perceived as sounds that make no sense; people are moving shapes of light and shadow, all appearing in a blur. You can't make out what you see or hear. Nothing has meaning, because past experiences can't help you. Your disorientation under such a circumstance results from a lack of recognition.

The recognition mode of perception occurs in the beginning of our active perceptual process. What we see depends as much on our memory of past perceptions as what we currently behold. In other words, recognition occurs at the intersection of perception and memory. We draw on images and ideas familiar to us. It's comforting and reassuring when we can make a connection of the past with the present.

In the term *recognition*, the *re* signifies "again," and *cognition* means "think." Together, recognition translates as seeing concurrently with eyes and mind, outwardly as well as inwardly, and is based on seeing once more what you have previously seen and known. In the recognition mode, we perceive visual elements as reminders of personal experiences. To give meaning to our vision, we selectively pull similar examples from our memory bank. In short, memory is an important function of recognition when experiences of the past and present appear momentarily juxtaposed. As a result, we experience a sense of control when we finally impose recognition on a visual statement, whereas we remain ill at ease in a terrain with objects we don't recognize.

Recognition is critical to the viewing process. When the unfamiliar outweighs the familiar, access through recognition is denied. The perceptual process is thwarted because you have no internal source for comparison. When an image or idea fails to conform to anything from personal experience, you experience difficulty registering what you're observing. In a social context, as long as you remain uninformed, you're prone to respond with ethnocentricity—a frame of mind that chafes at dealing with the unfamiliar, refuses to explore another's cultural context, and rejects further inquiry into or acknowledgment of cultural differences.

Ethnocentric vision can lead us to misinterpret circumstances that lie beyond the range of own particular belief system. We're often unconscious of having thus been programmed, and even of passing judgment that lacks validity. Because it is subconscious, this predisposition can't be felt by an uninformed bystander. This makes ethnocentricity difficult to identify and therefore to modify. Only increased knowledge or experience can dispel ethnocentricity. As is the case with orientation, when recognition is the primary perceptual modality we employ, we're oblivious to many aspects of the visual statement under observation.

Association and Expectation

Expectations define in advance what we want to see. The result of this preconditioning is that the viewer fails to engage in perceptive observation, but rather relies on memories as guideposts to frame the picture. If we come to a visual statement with a preconceived notion of what we should see, then these expectations will most likely alter our perception of what others see there. We edit what we see to fit the picture already present in our mind's eye. For example, in some countries, word of mouth touted the movie *The Exorcist* as the comedy hit of the season. Consequently, moviegoers laughed and called to the projectionist to play the most horrific scenes over and over again, upsetting others in the audience who were disposed to view the threatening aspect of the film—satanic possession—as a reality.

Because it's nearly impossible to maintain an emotionally neutral mind, we repeatedly approach reality with a situational frame of reference. But when we train ourselves in emotional neutrality, any visual statement can feed hungry eyes and act as a springboard for our creative imagination. Think of a more familiar situation: when frightened, we sense danger lurking everywhere; we make free associations and perceive everything in the surroundings as objects of potential aggression. In psychotherapeutic circles, therapists say that "any paranoid worth his salt can justify his paranoia."

Religious fanatics throughout history have warred against their rivals, all claiming that God was on their side. Religious persuasion comes with frames of reference that are part and parcel of respective faiths. Thus religious faith, like any emotionally charged expectation, shapes perception. Many members of "civilized" cultures have traditionally failed to accept others in their midst for their unique customs and beliefs; for example, North American indigenous peoples and the Ainu in Japan have long been perceived as "primitive" and treated with distain and rejection.

While the orientation mode perceives spatial relationships, and the recognition mode plays off memory of previous experiences, the association mode more directly evokes emotions. Hence, we judge objects, people, and ideas on the basis of our own belief system. The connections between what we could see and what our perceptions allow us to see are more tenuous than those between the optical reality and our previous experiences.

Having passed through stages in which associations and memories contribute to modify perception, we welcome the associative mode that projects these experiences onto our visual field in patterns that reaffirm our own belief system. We automatically look for familiar images and ideas. In the absence of previously known imagery, we manipulate visual statements by unknowingly adding or detracting aspects. Is it any wonder, then, how easily we superimpose inappropriate meanings in order to make them more relevant to our frame of reference?

Advertising and propaganda have made a science of courting our expectations that are rooted in religious, political, and personal experiences. Their ability to tap into the self-fulfilling prophecies that make us see only what we want to see largely defines their success. Although the association and expectation forms of perception are essential, these modes by themselves can frequently lead us to misinterpret what there is to see. Exposed to a visual statement that goes against our expectations, we might not think twice about rejecting or halting any further perceptual involvement.

To see what we're inclined to see is a universal phenomenon. When we're ready to rise above egocentrism and move on to more advanced modes of perception, however, we can see past our own belief system and develop a greater understanding of why we believe as we do. Then perhaps our tendency toward imagined superiority over the things we fail to understand will evaporate. We can then experience and practice cultural relativism without sacrificing our own beliefs. The price of cultural relativism need not be the loss of personally cherished values. But if we're content using only the first three subjective perceptual modes, we'll needlessly and unwittingly constrain our ability to see the world in a broader perspective.

Contemplation

Contemplation is a process of immersion. The contemplative mode draws as much on personal interpretations as on free associations. It allows us to look inward at the same time as seeking out details, in a climate of ease. Contemplation is a canvas for slipping into reverie. This perceptual mode represents an invitation to the visual statement to become a playing field for fantasy and imagination. A work of art may inspire us to intuit the poetic bond between the artist and the source of inspiration, or between the viewer and the visual statement, as the latter may simply serve as a starting place for satisfying creative musings. While being stimulated by what we're seeing, but not remaining limited by it, we open our imagination. Inspiration frequently springs from quiet contemplation. This experience leads us into a process in which we use what we see to imagine something else, thus editing and encoding the images while drawing upon our own visual memory bank.

Artists have long used a variety of means to induce the contemplative state. For example, Samuel Taylor Coleridge, who sought his muse in opium, complained that if he were interrupted while working, his inspiration and visions vanished, as occurred during the writing of his dream picture fragment, "Kubla Khan." For those lacking inspiration, Leonardo da Vinci had recommended gazing on drops of oil floating on water. Da Vinci knew from experience that contemplating on the strange configurations of the mix would inspire fertile eyes to conceive of new creative ideas. Another example is our childhood practice of seeing trolls or dragons in clouds. A direct contemplation of nature itself is a perfect focus for exploring what lies beyond the images, as William K. Mahony suggests: "The artist fashions his or her work of art by duplicating in the external world the contours of an inward vision." [2]

Empathy

Empathy is to see things from someone else's perspective, to put ourselves in someone else's shoes. Empathy means accepting and identifying with what we see; being involved, yet without sentimental overtones; sharing in mutual feelings; and seeing with compassion, while subordinating our inclination to take charge. Looking at something with empathy might answer the question of how to eliminate the distance between the self and the other, or how to position oneself as the other. An extreme example is a husband's stomach swelling in sympathy with his pregnant wife, known as "belly pregnancy." In other interpersonal relations there's a mutual understanding not to harm one another, for example, a mother's patience with her crying child, or a nonjudgmental psychiatrist with a patient. By comparing empathy with compassion, we get a clearer understanding of the nature of empathy. Both empathy and compassion involve feelings, but whereas empathy signifies an active emotional involvement with a person or a situation, compassion is more of a passive sympathetic concern.

Seeing Objectively

The main characteristics of objective perceptual modes are quite different from the subjective modes. In the objective modes we try to objectify our perceptions by keeping the personal and subjective at bay. The intent is to approach the visual field in a neutral and impersonal manner. Gertrude Stein's famous quote, "A rose is a rose is a rose," is technically accurate. However, when we see a rose do we simply see it as a flower, or do we imbue it with meaning? Whether a rose triggers pleasant or uncomfortable emotions in us, objective seeing requires us to filter out emotive associations.

In any situation, a viewer attempting to remain objective while gathering material must be alert to obstructions resulting from personal emotions and experiences. Consider the well-established unreliability of eyewitness reports in court cases. How many innocent people have been falsely accused on the basis of such reports? Though eyewitnesses report what they believe to be an objective truth, the disparity of accounts by multiple witnesses clearly demonstrates a lack of objectivity. These obstructions often surface from the unconscious and originate from personal loyalties and private agendas. Learning how to render objective accounts requires discipline, and we can't realistically expect objectivity from ourselves or anyone else without awareness of our capacity to unwittingly assign meaning to what we see.

The objective approach identifies two perceptual modes, observation and description, and analysis.

Observation and Description

Observation and description rely on logic rather than intuition. They require us to examine details non-judgmentally and verbalize them. This exercise itself requires a particular type of self-discipline. When you approach a visual field with objectivity, you're consciously attempting to step outside your emotional and intellectual frame of reference. You move from the general characteristics to the specific, while paying attention to every detail. At this stage of seeing, you make no attempt to choose between possible interpretations, and you experience no interaction with the visual statement; ideally, nothing is added and nothing is taken away. The goal here is to register the optical reality as accurately as possible. At this point a rose is just a rose. This is similar to a trained scientist recording the results of an experiment, or a detective noting evidence at a crime scene. By studying every detail of a scene, a private investigator must without bias record every bit of information, much like an investigative reporter takes notes before analyzing the meaning of an event.

A detailed and objective account of what you see might later give clues to the meaning, just as seemingly unimportant objects observed by the great fictional detective Sherlock Holmes became instrumental in his ability to solve crimes. Memory regularly plays tricks when you try to recall details of an object or a visual statement you've observed.

Analysis

Analysis is the next step of objective viewing. After observing a visual field, we engage in separating or breaking down the whole picture into its parts in order to register and examine the spatial relationships between properties of each element within the visual statement. Although we previously addressed questions of spatial relationships in discussing the subjective ways of seeing, we were talking about the relationship between the viewer and the object. Now we're talking about the relationship of each element in a visual statement to the others. Analyzing in this context involves deconstruction without interpretation.

Take for example a landscape painting with human figures. How large are the figures in relation to the rest of the landscape? Where in the painting are they placed? Is the degree of realism consistent throughout the painting? In other words, an analysis of a painting addresses each of its formal elements. Admittedly, objectively appraising a work of art is most demanding. In the following section we'll consider the difference between this type of objective discursive description and the process of interpretation.

Integrating Subjective and Objective Perception

So far, we've addressed the perceptual modes of seeing in the subjective and objective categories. We can access three additional perceptual modes by combining sensory and conceptual experiences: ordinary and creative meditation, discovery, and interpretation and assessment. These modes represent stages in which feelings and thoughts converge to form a basis for processing and interpreting the visual material we accumulate.

Ordinary and Creative Meditation

We've discussed contemplation as one of the subjective modes that we enter into lightly; meditation, which in its initial stage is quite similar to contemplation, progresses through additional levels of introspection and consciousness. When carried to its final stage, meditation can take the viewer into deeper insight, leading to an altogether altered state of mind. Meditation demands special concentration skills. The main difference between contemplation and meditation is that the former occurs entirely within a person's inner landscape, while successful meditation raises consciousness from the personal to the suprapersonal or transpersonal realm. Reality, whether communicated through language or through visual means, is realized through the perceptual modality of space and time. But a perceiver can escape the space-time continuum in altered states of consciousness, such as dreams, hallucinations, and/or meditation. Art exists on the boundary between these states, often subverting our *a priori* space-time expectations. Religious art, in particular, attempts to invest its statement in the representations of deities who communicate through otherworldly means by transcending time and space. Hence, we appropriate the religious icons that artists create to serve our own meditative practices.

A successful meditation session releases the viewer from self-consciousness, as well as from the images employed in the initial stages of the meditation sequence. Unless the person has the proper preparation and setting, he or she can spend hours in meditation and accomplish nothing. Meditation requires a quieting of all agitation and extraneous stimuli. Like going to sleep, it only happens if the internal and external conditions are right. Making them right is the first hurdle. Once the meditating individual aligns the body, mind, and spirit, everything begins converging into focus. Meditation affects and subtly alters subjective perception.

According to those who practice it, meditation mediates the distance between emotion and cognition, creating a healing power that restores inner balance to a distraught person. Artists, who often meditate as a way to look inward, reach a point of silence in which they can apply creative or imaginative visualization. With that frame of mind, any visual field can serve as a source of inspiration and act as a springboard for an individual creative agenda.

The experiences engendered from meditation vary from person to person. However, on some levels the narrative accounts of meditation experiences are surprisingly similar cross-culturally. In people's portrayal of an awareness that transcends the here and now, they reaffirm the sensation of being transported beyond time and space. For a viewer, meditation prepares for a unique perception, allowing what is seen its own existence. No matter who is doing the seeing—the artist who creates, or the viewer who merely seeks insight or freedom to dream—meditation deepens the experience for both.

Discovery

Unlike the religious viewer who comes to a visual statement looking for affirmation, other viewers may approach a visual field with open-ended expectations. When that's the case, the results are unpredictable. Seeing with a non-circumscribed frame of mind is referred to as seeing for the purpose of discovery, which is different from the recognition mode, since the latter is but a verification of things already known. Discovery, on the other hand, is a way of seeing in search of the unknown.

Pablo Picasso, who fully understood the uniqueness of the unexpected element inherent in discovery, said, "I search and I find, but not what I was searching for." To uncover new or unexpected aspects, we seek to acknowledge elements of images or ideas that are unforeseen. While feeling challenged, we remain accepting of what we're observing, even if we're unable to understand the visual statement. Discovery draws upon a positive response, whether what we see represents familiar terrain or not. The discovery mode builds on an attitude of being excited by challenge rather than discouraged by what seems foreign or incomprehensible. Discovery fosters an acceptance that is frequently the beginning of a self-perpetuating quest for more information about the specific cultural context.[3]

Interpretation and Assessment

Based on additional data garnered from questions regarding the context of the visual statement, we're now able to make an informed opinion. However, such opinions may yet be limited, because our sources of information are frequently one-sided and incomplete. Max Dimont pointed out that we tend to interpret history in standard ways; similarly, we can elicit relevant information by seeing an artwork from a religious perspective, a political perspective, a social perspective, and so on.[4] As any number of perspectives can be used to analyze any given material, who's to say which is the right approach? But if our aim is to broaden our visual perceptivity, we can't ignore our tendency to readily see what we expect to see and just as easily miss what we don't expect to see. Even if Sigmund Freud admitted that "sometimes a cigar is just a cigar," sometimes a cigar really is a phallic symbol. Sometimes it's a symbol of capitalistic arrogance, as Karl Marx might have seen it. Ask Fidel Castro, and he might tell you it's a symbol of national pride. Until we sensitize ourselves otherwise, we as viewers are susceptible to this "self-fulfilling prophecy" phenomenon to the degree that we share the artist's religious, political, or social persuasion.

As is often the case, the whole exceeds the sum of its parts when we combine the recollection of our initial subjective experiences with our added objective experiences. Sometimes we have several different subjective experiences that then can be integrated into something objective through processing additional information. For example, a healthy child, when very young, has the subjective experience of having both a wonderful mommy and a hateful mommy. In the mind of the child, the two mommies are separate people until maturity allows their reconciliation into one person.

Interfacing emotive and rational responses between the encoding and decoding processes solidifies the aesthetic experience. What was previously a subjective perception primarily based on taste becomes an informed assessment anchored in emotive and rational experiences. As Ludwig Wittgenstein observed, "We see the world the way we do, not because that is the way it is, but because we have these ways of seeing."[5]

Seldom does a person consciously engage all of the ways of seeing described above. We tend to favor those modes that we've grown accustomed to using in given situations. But in addressing visual statements, be they nature, people, or works of art, we can objectify our perceptions by understanding and training our faculties. A blend of the emotional and the conceptual perceptual modes greatly enhances perceptual experience.

Ideally, we'll experience optimal perceptual awareness when we inform our initial emotional responses with rational, intellectual, and conceptual modalities, then integrate them into our viewing patterns. The "Ten Modes of Perception" exercise in appendix A on page 128 will guide you through the process of identifying the perceptual modes you use automatically, and deliberately engaging the modes that you tend to ignore.

No two people see in exactly the same way, even when looking at the same event. Who we are influences how we see and how we interpret what we see. It's not what there is to be seen that's most decisive in perception, but who is doing the seeing. In addition to having selective memory and recall, all of us see selectively. Truly, the poets through the ages have been right all along—it's all in the eyes of the beholder.

Understanding Visual Memory

Since everyday living is filled with too many visual inputs, a person adapts selectively to each individual situation. When we're in familiar surroundings, mental habits and experience step in to guide us through the maze of the visual onslaughts.

In preelectric cultures unencumbered by radio or television, people sought mental stimulation in activities such as leisure time, religion, festivals, storytelling, and letter writing. Response to non-visual entertainment in those days depended on the initiative of individual imagination. In other words, each person became actively involved with synthesizing visualizations based in self-generated mental images. Through oral traditions, most aspects of the universe were made comprehensive and committed to memory in the form of stories that everybody knew and recanted.

In view of modern lifestyles characterized by excessive TV watching that limits the occasion for more challenging participatory activities, some ancient cultural pursuits have become obsolete. Entertainment today is largely equated with passive consumption. From childhood on, TV programs transfer their typical prepackaged format of sex and violence directly into the mind of the viewer, leaving little time for genuine analysis and little room for detailed memories.

However, in spite of technological innovations, some people do retain an aptitude for visual memory and develop it further. Artists are among those who create, based in part on a repository of recorded visual images. The artists' proclivity lies in their ability to project visual memories, and transform and materialize them through creative energy and technical skills into new creations. Artists draw upon stored memories of previously seen works of art and integrate selected aspects of these memories into new and original creations.

Responding to visual data and storing images for retrieval from a memory bank are basic to survival. Some memories or images remain on the precognitive level and function as a motivating force in an unconscious reaction/action paradigm. Many aspects of how we learn to remember and how memory operates are not yet fully understood. It would be helpful if we had a finite answer to the question of which processes facilitate the recognition, storage, and recollection of sensory information. The process of encoding and decoding, which explains the transformation of sensory information into a memory representation, and the formation of a memory code remain central research topics in cognitive psychology.

Eidetic memory is a relevant concept here, although the term generates a broad range of interpretation. (At this writing, a quick Google search yielded 490,000 search results.) For the purpose of our discussion, I define eidetic memory as a distinguishing feature of people who are innately gifted in image recall. Eidetic images distinguish themselves as self-generated "mind pictures," or visualizations culled from memory, independent of the presence of ocular perception or exterior stimuli. To illustrate, in the 1940s when Europeans started to trade with some Inuit tribes near Furbisher Bay in Northern Canada, they found that the Eskimos had retained the oral tradition transmitted from generation to generation to the extent that they could describe in minute detail the visit of an explorer ship from the early 1600s. This recall included a credible drawing of the name of the vessel. I say "drawing," because these individuals had never seen a written language in their lives and had no idea of its meaning.

Studies of elementary school children show that eidetic ability is strong in younger children but decreases with age. Researchers explain this phenomenon by suggesting that the eideticism faculty is displaced by developing language capabilities. But this explanation doesn't seem altogether credible. Consider the thousands of characters required to command the Chinese written language. From an early age a Chinese child must progressively memorize a minimum of two thousand characters to achieve functional literacy. Writing a single character requires from one to thirty brush or pen strokes. With such training, it's no wonder that Chinese students develop excellent memorization skills. On this level, eidetic memory development approaches what we could consider photographic memory.

Most of us have the potential for eidetic recall. With practice, we can expand our visual memory bank so that the path between image and memory is shortened. Exercising visual memory can enhance our retention and recall of perceptions, no matter which modality of seeing we use. Furthermore, verbalizing the visual experience transforms it to a cognitive experience, setting the stage for repeated recall, independent of the initial context. In this process, memory becomes a tool, facilitating *recontextualization* as we encounter new visual experiences that transform or even supersede the memories of older experiences. To experience how verbal descriptions can stimulate your senses and sharpen your ability to remember details, try the "Visual Memory" experiment in appendix A on page 129. The experiment is designed to demonstrate how consciously processing your visualization by verbalizing the experience makes it easier to recall an accurate memory of a visual statement. Purposeful observation optimizes your perception.

Memory is the agent that preserves the hard-won knowledge we gain from life experiences—it's what connects us to reality as we see it. Associating a memory of a past experience with a new situation, by way of recognizing familiar aspects in each, is itself a creative process. A memory, in other words, is an artistic rendering of an experience. The following chapter focuses on the way artists use accrued memories as a palate of associative and comparative materials to create new experiences.

2

Decoding Art

Based on the premise that all art is the aesthetic counterpart to a culture's ethos, and that the ethics and values of a culture in turn stem from this, visual literacy inherently entails more than just accessing information. It means that we must come to the visual statement with some meaningful questions to be able to interpret its potential as communication.

In the preceding chapter we focused on developing visual skills. Chapter 2 will train our focus on art as a type of visual field as well as a repository of refined cultural interpretations. In the "Encountering a Work of Art" section below we'll discuss art as both a form of communication and a method of inquiry.

As the most expressive exponent of a culture's identity, art is a synthesis of the visionary and the rational, functioning for society much as dreams do for the individual. Through visual expressions, artists reflect latent tensions and aspirations in anticipation of more overt expressions in their contemporary social and political arenas. Art makes it possible for us to experience the world through eyes other than our own. We'll examine art not as an art historian would, but as explorers who discover in art a guide to an understanding of the culture from which it comes. From this perspective we can see art as the manifestation of a collective dream—a psychic document.

This chapter will also address the problems related to the interpretation of art, and how they hinge on the viewer. The scientific process contends that an observer can't observe without altering what is seen. Similarly, of greatest importance among the many variables that come into play in interpretation of art are the artist's intent and the beholder's imaginative range. A case in point is da Vinci's *Mona Lisa*: there's no way a modern viewer will see this painting in the same way as the artist who created it or as his contemporary viewers did. A question that frequently comes to mind is, where do artists get their inspiration? The answer depends on the time period and the culture to which the artists belong. Scholars believe that the cave and rock paintings of early civilizations were inspired by fear of and dominance over wildlife that was both threatening and necessary for survival. In later societies, religion became the greatest source of inspiration. More recently it was nature. Today, nature has been marginalized and replaced by the culture of technocracy.

What all artists have in common is their usage of existing art. This art inspires them to know both *what* and *how* they want to create, as well as what they don't want to create. Artists and artisans alike derive their world view from the culture in which they grew up. Hence, they apply symbols and style in the context of shared culture-specific experiences. In traditional cultures in particular, the majority of art is inspired by religion that in turn affords a prime connection between the psyche of the people and their visual culture. From time immemorial, artists have devoted their creativity to moral education as means of provoking discourse on social issues. On the receiving end, some consumers experience art as a profitable investment; for others, art simply offers a source of mental stimuli, even joy.

Since art is the focus in this chapter, we'll examine the extent to which one of the central concepts in art studies, the aesthetic, has changed over time. For the Greeks, the criteria for excellence in visual arts were the same as those for poetry and prose. Aristotle viewed art as anything that expressed beauty, harmony, and truth. Eighteenth-century German philosopher and educator Alexander Baumgarten reclassified aesthetics as a separate branch of philosophy. Since the early 20th century, aesthetics has been defined as any visual statement eliciting an emotional response. The dependence of art criticism on the age-old method of literary criticism has never been severed.

Inspired by Einstein's theory of relativity, the changing definition of art paralleled the change from the prior concept of art as defined by canons, to the idea of inclusiveness. Normative standards practiced for centuries were no longer valid; the new point of view proclaimed that anything goes—be it pleasing or ugly or shocking, it's all art.

Modern art came to represent a movement advocating "art for art's sake," proclaiming that art doesn't need to have a purpose beyond its mere existence. This unconventional attitude states that a work of art has its own *raison d'être*, and as such has neither reason nor obligation to be anything other than itself. Art movements created under such an aegis reflect Western culture-specific values in response to the turmoil at the onset of the 20th century.

When viewing the art of an unfamiliar culture, we're unlikely to understand the value system from which the artwork was created. Since each culture has its own aesthetic ideals and subject matter, as long as we appreciate the basic fact that interpretations change according to cultural contexts, simply analyzing the formal aspects of the art, taking it at face value, is acceptable. This approach works for those who put unfamiliar art under a familiar umbrella, viewing it through the filter of their own cultural values. But we'll gain deeper insight through the 20th century's greatest shift in perspective—quantum reasoning—which states that things change in accordance with a viewer's changing vantage point.

In early traditional societies, art was expected to express moral values in visual terms. By expressing values inherent in the dominant religious institutions, art functioned as reminders of these values. A mutual agreement between the patron, the employer, and the artists or craftsmen who lived for the acceptance of their work, was reached by applying long-established artistic conventions. These conventions ensured continuity with traditions through the practice of the accepted aesthetic language of their time. Yet artists of the Classical, Medieval, and Renaissance periods gloried in tweaking the old rules. Modernist artists of the 20th century upped the ante by claiming complete freedom of expression, negating traditional conventions that *de facto* limited the freedom of expression. Freedom to invent new rules has since been seen as mandatory for the realization of the ultimate creative process. This freedom pertains to every aspect of creativity, especially in experimenting with new media. Contemporary artists make it their business to pose questions rather than answer them. We'll discuss the changing premises of 21st century art in more detail in chapter 5.

In the postmodern art movement, artists are neither beholden to a sponsor nor to a public, but only to themselves and their faithfulness to truth as they see it. Artists leave the public to comprehend art in any way the public pleases. Today, viewers are responsible for uncovering questions inherent in the work, for which there are no definitive answers. We must all individually decide what we want to know and tailor our own questions accordingly—even if the answers vary in degree of credibility.

Encountering a Work of Art

Fine arts generally invite and welcome our eyes to participate in the challenge of understanding more than we already do. In the words of Picasso, "art is a lie that brings us closer to the truth." Personally, I would add, "...and closer to life itself." To the extent that we can afford, we surround ourselves with art that engages our imagination in continuous dialogue. A painting acts like a mirror, reflecting our temporary state of mind, time and again making us revise what we are seeing. Artists create visualizations of emotions and concepts, and the viewers themselves also become artists, as they do the same when encountering the work.

Though this idea—that every time we look at a painting we're in fact re-creating it—may seem strange for now, by the end of this chapter it will become self-evident. When we come to understand the perceptual process, we learn to break artwork into identifiable components and address them in their respective aspects, both independently and, finally, holistically. Extracting the maximum meaning from a work of art only happens through a process of diligent commitment. Casual viewers on the other hand won't always aspire to see all that there is to be seen in every work of art.

Let's take a look at how the sightseeing public behaves when visiting a traditional museum, an avant-garde New York gallery, or Elvis Presley's Graceland. These venues tend to provide labels next to their displays intended to help viewers identify what they are looking at. Most sightseers will only briefly stand in front of a work of art before their eyes are inevitably drawn to the museum label that lists the title of the piece, name of the artist, year created, and other relevant information. Then a dance follows, the eyes jumping from label to picture and back to the label. Though the information supplied is relevant, it overtakes the artwork itself, distracting the viewer from actively experiencing the visual statement—the artwork itself. This experience is more intellectual than emotional, robbing the viewer of a deeper, more holistic aesthetic experience.

The problem with the museum label is that its information pertains only to context—the secondary, or *etic,* aspects of the painting. What the label can't address is the most important aspect of the work, that is, its primary, or *emic,* aspects, including the formal elements and artistic essence. When we allow ourselves to be sidetracked by context, the aesthetic qualities that otherwise would go uncensored, speaking straight to the heart, are sidetracked. That's why it's preferable to at first simply look at a work of art and let it stimulate you emotionally while you engage the subjective ways of seeing. You then have the opportunity to begin an interior dialogue with the work and contemplate it by immersing yourself to the extent you consider it worth your while, before proceeding with a more systematic and objective analysis. A growing number of museums now place labels further from the works in order to encourage more active engagement by the viewers.

Signage belongs to the most rudimentary form of visual language, constituting the lowest common denominator of visual communication. A composite of several signs goes into the making of an image, and an image sometimes functions as a symbol. A seasoned viewer recognizes the presence of an image that is intended to carry symbolic meaning from the way the image is presented. Such an image usually has assumed a form that seems out of context in relation to its surroundings.

The least accessible aspect of an artwork is its symbols. Some viewers are symbol-blind, just as some individuals are color-blind. Symbols are not universally understood; they're culture-specific. A symbol represents an idea for which a chosen image is created and specifically fashioned to effectively serve as a reminder of that idea, the meaning of which transcends its visual appearance. In fact, in order to convey that a symbol is intended to function as a symbol, the artist frequently renders it on a level of abstraction inconsistent with the level of abstraction in the rest of the painting. As shorthand expressions containing references to ideas that otherwise would be cumbersome to spell out, symbols communicate economically. Take for example the symbolic affectivity of the cross. The cross is a symbol that carries deeply felt connotations among Christians, yet it's not automatically comprehended among non-Christians. Moreover, the visual appearance of one and the same symbol can mean different things in different cultures. The swastika is an example of a symbol that changes meaning depending upon its cultural context: in Hopi culture, it means happy harvesting; in Hindu culture, it's a fertility symbol, and in Buddhism, it refers to the sun or light. Of course, everyone in the West is familiar with Hitler's swastika—though only slightly altered with the spikes depicted in reverse direction, it looks very similar to the others. Hitler's swastika, however, stands in deep contrast to the message of sun, light, and fertility, and reminds us of the Nazis' belief in the Aryan superrace and their deadly anti-Semitic convictions.

When attempting to understand a symbol, we should approach it from two separate perspectives: first, from the perspective of its iconography—its visual appearance; and second, for the purpose of understanding its iconology—the meanings the respective cultures have conferred upon it.[1] In our exploration of the meaning of works of art, we'll use a strategy that addresses the art from two separate perspectives: the emic and the etic. The former perspective deals with visual aspects only, including an examination of the formal elements such as space, line, color, and so on. The latter perspective, the etic, examines the art in context, including the artist's background and the broader cultural context of place and time—the type of information supplied in a museum label.

The integration and synchronization of the emic (visual) and the etic (contextual) information is of utmost importance, yet, as we'll discuss in more detail below, it doesn't necessarily simplify the interpretive process. After exploring multiple interpretations, we face one of the most difficult challenges, that there is no one correct interpretation. Culture-specific differences are discernable in both the emic and etic aspects, and we need to view them with sensitivity. Though formal aesthetic elements are universal, artists employ them from their own cultural traditions and aesthetic preferences. While art is the visual manifestation of an artist's commentary on his or her time, society, and culture, it's fallacious to expect art to speak for itself. It can't.

Identifying Visual Aspects

In the previous section we touched on the reciprocal process of creating and viewing, and on the relationship between artist and beholder. Does the expected viewing audience determine what and how the artist will create? In the past, artists were commissioned to work for religious institutions or wealthy patrons, resulting in the reflection of the employers' tastes and preferences in the final product. But the world of art has changed. Contemporary artists, without a specified audience, and more often than not lacking sponsors, must act in their own interest and as their own public relations agent when it comes to exhibiting and selling their works. Therefore, their works often take on a "to-whom-it-may-concern" quality. This attitude isn't entirely without precedent, however. An old Sanskrit text of Indian aesthetic theory, *rasa* (essence), posits that the artist and viewer participate in the same process. The artist creates ideal representations preserved in his or her visual memory bank as mind-pictures by projecting these into visual manifestations in the appropriate medium (the material used to create the artwork). It's the responsibility of the viewers who belong to the same culture as the artist, and have similarly stored memories of the ideal, to see the ideal in the work of art. Whether the art they see comes close to the ideal or not is the viewer's problem, not the artist's.

In the maze of various kinds of art we encounter today, we as viewers must know what to look for and which questions to ask to make sense of them. When facing a painting, the first question we should ask ourselves is, "What do I want to see?" Unlike the constraints imposed on the experience of reading, with words neatly following each other like an army marching across the page in single file, art meets the eyes in an instantaneous flash. This is the *coup d'oeil*, a unique experience that strikes all at once in a first impression. At this point we're responding with the subjective ways of seeing, which allow us to emotionally experience the work's aesthetic flavor. We should allow this first impression to settle, and deposit it as a special moment in our memory bank.

After engaging the subjective ways of seeing, we're prepared to proceed to the next question: "What do I want to know?" We approach our answer to this question using the objective ways of seeing, first by looking at the material aspects of the work such as size and medium—the type of information stated on the museum label. Then we give a detailed verbal description of the painting's components, starting with the general characteristics and moving to the specific. The purpose of this description is to ensure that we've registered each and every element of the work.

Next, we look for symbols or iconographic elements, recognizing them by their eye-catching qualities and unexpected visual appearance. When compared to the rest of the elements in a work of art, a symbol seems different and incongruent, both in terms of style and format. Note that we haven't yet attempted to interpret the meaning of the symbols or the subject matter. That's our next step.

After our description is complete, we move on to the analysis, which occurs in two phases, the emic and the etic. The emic phase concerns the visual aspects and addresses the question of how the artist has rendered them. We proceed with an analysis of the formal elements, also known as the *artistic means* or *visual vocabulary* artists work with, such as space, line, color, form, etc. Artists achieve aesthetic unity in a work by successfully manipulating each of the formal elements, which function as building blocks in the total structure of the painting. We as viewers come to the finished product through a process of deconstructing each of the formal elements, and in this way connect with the artist by re-creating the artwork through inverting the creative process. (For a brief outline of the building blocks, see the "Guide to the Formal Elements" in appendix B on page 136.)

The artist employs each of these formal elements with an understanding of its potential capabilities and limitations. Which formal elements take priority depends on many variables including the artist's chosen style, context, and medium, as well as the time and purpose of creation. In traditional works, the order of importance given to the formal elements was more or less preordained depending on the time and place. Modern and postmodern art may appear less predictable and more challenging to decipher, especially since the artist's vocabulary has expanded with the introduction of new media, including multimedia or mixed media. Nevertheless, the Indian *rasa* still applies: it's the artist who creates the work, but it's the viewer who sees it.

Interpreting Contextual Aspects

Up to this point in our discussion of decoding art, we've only dealt with deconstructing the visual aspects of an artwork through emic analysis. The second part of our analysis, the etic phase, answers the *who, when, where,* and *why* questions. Because visual perception is more than merely seeing, in addition to acknowledging an artwork's emic aspects we need to look at the context in which the artist created the work, in terms of time and place. As one of my students observed, "You can no longer be content with what you see on the surface; you have to dig with your mind until you find what lies behind. It's like having a one-to-one discussion with the art object." Seeing a work of art ideally leads to a genuine appreciation based on a cognitive understanding of the complexity of the creative process.

Following our deconstruction of emic aspects, we're ready to put the artwork back together in the context of what we discover from the artist's circumstances, a process called *reconstruction.* In this multifaceted reconstruction phase, we can enjoy blending our first impression with what we've since learned about the work from the various perspectives we'll now explore. Our challenge is to integrate the optical aspects of the work with the information gathered, interfacing with and consuming the artwork anew.

Etic analysis requires researching information pertaining to sociocultural determinants, and artistic conventions and practices including time and place. A viewer's identity determines the role of the etic aspects of a work. Most likely, a viewer who shares the culture of the artist will understand the language and the symbols of that culture. This viewer's experience with the artwork will consequently be deeper and quite different from that of a viewer from a different culture. (For a brief description of art analysis, see the "Guide to Analyzing a Work of Art" in appendix C on page 143.)

Interpreting meaning and evaluating relevance obtained through etic analysis from a non-ethnocentric perspective is anything but easy. Just as the visual, emic elements are interdependent, so also are the etic elements. The *who, when, where,* and *what* of an artwork must be understood in context of their mutual dependence. As with the emic aspects, the whole is more than the sum of its parts. The *who* refers to the artist, and familiarity with his or her biography gives the viewer an understanding of motivating influences and a greater insight into the work. In attempting to view the artist and the work from historic *(when)* and cultural *(where)* perspectives, we focus on the original context. The answers to the *when* and *where* reveal the function of art at a particular point in time in the history of the culture in question.

The style of an artwork also reflects the *when* and *where.* Style is to art as dialect is to language; it's the catalyst that unifies cultural expressions and identifies the aesthetics of a given historical period. Style identifies schools of art as well as individual artists. Repetition in art over an extended period of time can lead to the development and identity of a particular style. This process, however, is not chiseled in stone, and undergoes change in response to specific cultural conditions, such as

- technical innovations
- confluence of art from different cultures as encouraged by trade
- natural disasters
- wars
- changes in economic conditions and political status of nations
- variances in levels of political/religious fervor.

Another tipping point occurs when artists become so well versed in a particular style that their works, though they may approach technical perfection, are no more than repetitions of earlier works, devoid of emotional impact. At this point, the style is in entropy and is ripe for organic change, which can mean either decline or rejuvenation. Some of the causes that explain why styles in art change are quite similar to theories pertaining to culture changes in general, as we'll discuss in more detail in chapter 4.

Subject matter is sometimes used as a facile way of identifying style, such as in Western still life paintings. Other genres in traditional Western art are narratives relating to historic events and figures. These narratives depict religious, political, and cultural stories, each with their own messages. Subject matter in traditional Indian paintings, in the format of miniature paintings for example, were visual enactments of their ancient myths and legends. An outsider of either culture who is unfamiliar with their respective stories wouldn't understand the depicted narrations, nor recognize the presence of symbols (iconography) or their meaning (iconology).

While it's relatively easy to recognize the presence of symbols, to understand their meanings requires cultural insight. This is particularly important when viewing religious art. Religiously inspired paintings function as visual texts for preliterate laypeople, as reminders of their culture's code of ethics and cultural values. Their purpose, in other words, is didactic across all traditional cultures.

Landscapes are the preferred subject matter in Chinese and Japanese traditional paintings. These paintings are to some extent also religious, inasmuch as the depiction of space reflects religious traditions of both Buddhism and Taoism. A viewer unfamiliar with the religious traditions is unlikely to grasp the subtleties inherent in this genre.

Unless the artist has named the work or given it a caption, the collector, museum, or gallery will usually supply a title. Throughout the world, captions traditionally functioned as means to orient the viewer by pointing to the right direction through identifying the subject matter, by citing an objective historic reference, or by coining a poetic title. Contemporary artists frequently leave the work untitled, or in some cases provide a label that has no bearing on the subject matter of the painting itself. At times the artist simply titles a work with the intent of confusing the viewer. This ploy underscores artists' attempts to withhold information, encouraging the art work to speak purely through its visual medium.

When works of art are displayed in museums or other venues far removed in time and place from their original settings, they're viewed in a new context. This new context, though unintended by the artist, gives new meaning to the work. This is a type of recontextualization, which is a key aspect of the reconstruction process.

Museum labels serve as a short reminder of the work's original sociohistoric context, both helping and hindering the viewer. Though the labels for the most part provide accurate information, they fail to alert the viewers of the implications of recontextualization.

An additional recontextualization takes place when serious viewers seek interpretations rendered by professional art critics who inevitably also infuse their own recontextualization. Consider how the Bible and well-known works of literature have been interpreted and reinterpreted over time. Works of art share a similar fate when viewed cross-culturally.[2]

The fact that each culture expresses its art in its own culture-specific ways necessarily renders some of the etic perspectives we've discussed less applicable in some cases. Before we modify interpretations of art from cultures other than our own, we must be sensitive and adjust our approach on a case-by-case basis, and pose questions appropriate to the specific culture under investigation. There's ample room for misinterpretation when we're unfamiliar with the culture in question. As

Confucius advised, when crossing a river, take your time, go slowly, and feel each stone step by step.

Negotiating Authoritative Interpretations

In order to welcome viewers of their work to participate in the construction of meaning, some artists might provide hints that allude to intended ambiguities. Others refuse to offer any comment on the meaning of their work, as talking about it would decrease its stature as art. In their opinion, if a work of art needs to be explained it has failed in its capacity as art, whose unique contribution is its ability to communicate precisely where words fail.

A work of art is more interesting when it allows room for individual interpretation. When left open-ended, without the artist's insistence upon a singular correct interpretation, the work is our invitation to accept responsibility for viewing the piece and generating our own meaning from it. But a problem emerges when we're left to our own interpretations: though we're capable of training a critical eye on the artists' perceptions and interpretations, we often forget to apply the same critical acumen to our own perceptions and interpretations. How do we make sense of the multiple interpretations we summon when studying a work of art? We can strengthen our own analysis by setting aside our personal frame of reference and reconsidering our comprehension in regard to interpretations belonging to expert viewers. Our interpretations of a work of art depend on our personal recontextualization as well as others'. We must exercise patience and suspend judgment until we've reexamined the work from a number of different expert perspectives.

Of course, we don't need to take the commentary of critics at face value any more than we would the commentary of the artists themselves. In evaluating the opinions of professional art critics, make sure to validate their credentials by investigating their background, education, and primary culture (remember that critics don't automatically speak the visual language of cultures outside of their own). Also be aware that credible art critics reveal the criteria they apply in judging the relative excellence of the work under review. Finally, we set ourselves up for disappointment if we expect the experts to take unified positions among themselves; after all, no two critics see the same work of art in exactly the same light, so to speak. Even among experts, interpretations can vary widely according to preferred critical perspectives. What follows is a brief description of some of the most common of these critical perspectives, that of the artist, the anti-artist, the historian, the feminist, and finally, the viewer.

Artist Perspective

This school of thought insists that the artist provides the most authentic source of the meaning of the artwork. From this standpoint, it's essential to examine the artist and the art in the numerous alternative contexts in which they function. If the art is an extension of the artist, then the artist must also be examined in relation to the intended audience. Finally, the present work must be viewed in the context of previous works—those created both by the artist and by his or her contemporaries.

From this perspective, we view a work of art from the hands of a famous artist with a different set of expectations and trust than we would work produced by an unknown artist. Consider a sketch by Picasso. Visually it could be quite unimpressive and consist of but a few lines. But if some of those lines represent an authenticated signature, Picasso's sketch is highly prized compared to a similar sketch created by a lesser-known artist. In other words, what really counts is not so much *what* is created as *who* created it. The artist-centered view places a premium on credibility in terms of name recognition. Suppose, for example, the mayor of your home town declares, "I will end the war in Iraq," and the White House issues the same statement. Which would carry more weight? Obviously, we tend to take the *who* more seriously than the *what.*

Anti-Artist Perspective

This view claims that anything an artist has to say about his or her intended message is irrelevant. The thinking here is that artists' objectives don't necessarily correspond to what they succeed in expressing in their work, and even when pressed to explain, they're prone to speak more to what they'd wanted to articulate than to what they actually accomplished. Additionally, they could already be thinking ahead to their next creations and what they hope to express in them. As such, an artist's commentary on his or her own work is unreliable at best, misleading at worst.

Regardless, in allowing a work to go public, the artist releases the work and cuts the umbilical cord, giving it a life of its own.

Historical Perspective

Historical contexts help us understand the role artists played in their time. In a traditional society, artists were employed by a patron. A patron could be an institution, religious or otherwise, or a private person. The relationship between the patron, the artist, and the audience is relatively clear. In this hierarchical structure, money equaled power, and patrons used artists to "speak" for them; hence, it was really the patrons who had the final authority. The artists' sole function was to follow the given directives.[3]

Feminist Perspective

Feminists posit that, in keeping with patriarchal values, society as a whole institutionalizes sexism in art. Since the 1970s, women have published reinterpretations of arts in general and of specific artworks from a feminist perspective.

A key consideration in the feminist view is economic. Though all artists in the early stages of their professional lives invest an unreasonable amount of time and energy searching for exhibition space, female artists have encountered more obstacles and experienced less institutional cooperation than their male counterparts. After they find a gallery or alternative space to exhibit their art, the challenge remains to elicit professional reviews. Though there are a few men who claim to be feminists, until recently the established critics, primarily male, considered the feminist movement countercultural and largely ignored their message. Several prominent female art critics have written essays and books exploring the legitimacy of an identifiable feminine aesthetic that distinguishes itself in terms of subject matter, imagery, and medium.

While the unique commitment of women as child bearers and nurturers is readily acknowledged by even the most conservative men, they still widely reject that assumption that women's art mirrors an interpretation of a gender-specific world view. This circumstance has led many women to claim that they no longer need male validation to assure their position of importance, or to challenge the public to question the old assumptions that women are inferior and that men should define the norm and thereby present their art as gender-neutral.

Another under-researched question is how gender influences viewers' perception of the artwork and its subject matter, particularly when the subject matter focuses on the female. Throughout time, the female form, whether clothed or nude, has been a predominant subject in art around the world. We could logically assume that men have a different take on the female nude than women who may see the same nude in feminist terms, in that a male viewer probably responds to the aesthetics of the painting in a similar manner as to the sensuality of the woman's naked body, that is, from an experiential perspective.

Do women look at such paintings only from an aesthetic point of view, or do they see an alluring, naked female body, explicitly expressing sexuality? Does a woman identify with that image? As further food for thought, what if the artist were revealed to be a woman rather than an assumed man—would this produce a different agenda for both the artist and the viewer?

Viewer Perspective

No matter the perspective from which we view art, the values, knowledge, principles, and theories we ascribe to it are in constant flux. Our perception changes as our knowledge grows. Artists, who have invested their skills and time to create, expect viewers to become dynamic partners and invest equally in the process. What we take from a work of art is proportional to what we invest in it. Yet the dialogue between the viewer and the viewed remains unresolved in terms of a singular translation. David Danow suggests a reason for this in stating that "the structure of the work of art is part the intentionality of both creator and perceiver." He further cited Jan Mukarovsky's comparison of "the evolution of the arts to an uninterrupted dialogue between encoders and decoders, between all those who successively create and all those who successively perceive art."[4]

No single interpretation holds primacy over another, as long as the artwork remains an open-ended challenge to alternative interpretations. We as viewers should also remain open to suggestion, yet have the courage to pursue our personal opinions. In the words of one of my students, "Never be ashamed of the right to look at something and think what you want."

Unlike artists, who begin with *tabula rasa*—an empty slate or canvas—and end up with a work of art, viewers start with the finished product, and move through the creative layers, as if re-creating in reverse. The artist constructs; the viewer deconstructs, reconstructs, and recontextualizes.

Each generation redefines art in its own way, anew, over and over again. Consider da Vinci's *Mona Lisa*: twenty-first century viewers of this work will have a different response from the original 16th-century viewers. We should be at ease with the fact that a work of art will engender different responses from different people at different times. No one experiences a work of art exactly as another does.

In this book we've frequently referred to mental habits and tried to explain how we get locked into habitual manners of using our eyes. This discussion serves as a reminder that what we see depends on how we use our eyes, and reciprocally, how we use our eyes depends on what we already know.

An artwork in and of itself is never final. It's human to feel uncomfortable having so many options. While it's difficult to acknowledge the many justifiable options, it's equally difficult to assume the responsibility of forming our own interpretation and allowing it to be, for us, the most valid. Figure for example to what extent our ethical values influence how we view art. This is apparent in the appreciation of a work of art from our own culture, and even more so from across cultures.[5]

Now we face a potential dilemma: interfacing emotive and rational responses between all of our encoding and decoding should solidify the aesthetic experience—but does it? What was previously a subjective opinion primarily based on taste, becomes, on account of our subsequent accumulated knowledge, an informed assessment anchored in our alliance of emotive and rational understanding. The danger lies in sacrificing our aesthetic pleasure for rational probing. Many treasured poems from childhood have inadvertently been stripped of their original impact of pure aesthetic pleasure when schoolteachers analyzed the multiple meanings inherent in the poem. As the poem was deconstructed, its luster was lost.

Are we committing the same offense in this discussion? Does deeper knowledge really enhance our appreciation of the artwork, or does it detract? Can our aesthetic perception survive the exposure to rational analyses? Will it change? If so, how?

We can answer these legitimate theoretical concerns by turning once again to the artwork and leaning on our memory to retrieve our original impression as we experienced it in that first encounter. Maybe we'll be surprised to see that, after exploring the work and understanding its context from every possible point of view, the work itself has literally transformed our first impression. As a rule, when creative energies intermingle, miracles can happen. This should make us even more curious. James N. Wood, director of the J. Paul Getty Trust, probably described the phenomenon best: "Art is a mystery: if you think you have cracked it you are either arrogant or ignorant!"

Responding to Culture-Specific Aesthetics

Multicultural visual literacy is of particular importance today because we live in a multicultural world. Regardless of where the work originated, a work of art is framed by the cultural context in which it was created. Active seeing demands that we step beyond our own cultural frame of reference and beyond our comfort zone of the art so familiar to us since birth.

When we address a work of art from our own culture and examine the emic and etic aspects, the same approach applies to cross-cultural viewing. Inasmuch as contemporary art reflects the world views of artists of our time, traditional art is anchored in a corresponding ethic of the culture that produced it.

Understanding traditional art of another culture involves a viewing process that is even more complex, since the depth of understanding is determined by who the viewer is and the extent of his or her multicultural horizon. Cross-cultural viewers are subject to the same variables as those discussed above. We've learned that, in its broadest sense, context confers meaning contingent on the culture, place, gender, education, and experience of the viewer. In the very act of examining a work of art, the viewer engages in a recontextualization that reflects the multicultural maturity of the viewer.

Let's consider examples from non-Western art. We've seen that in certain cultures artists have preferences for specific media and subject matter; by examining the art and recognizing in it a specific cultural aesthetic, we'll see how this aesthetic is a manifestation of that culture's ethics.

Frequently we can find works that are so close to perfection that we, as well as people from the originating cultures, consider them true representatives of the art of their culture. For example, Indian art is best known to the Western public for its religious sculptures, yet most of us are obliged to view it in museums, away from the original context. These sculptures were initially placed on the facade of temple walls and could be seen as if emanating from the inside of the temple, crowding the outside walls. Hindu sculptures most frequently depicted exemplary renditions of sensuous, nearly nude female figures, alone or at times in conjunction with male figures. Throughout the history of Indian art, the fertility cult was matched with symbols conveying the creative fusion of female and male, *shakti* and *shakta,* energies. Erotic sculpture, for which the temples at Khajuraho and Konarak have become famous, personifies the intersection between gods and humans. The creative act of procreation, consummated by the union of shakti and shakta, symbolically represents humans in interplay with the divine. The religious aspect of Indian sculpture focuses on deities, using human type-forms (that is, their most characteristic aspects) or generic versions of the human form, reflecting the Indian centeredness on the inter-relationship between gods and humans.

In China, with a tradition that shies away from nudity, *Shan Shui* (landscape painting) is the preeminent art form that in the eyes of Western viewers has become the stereotypical representation of Chinese art. These paintings have two major components: *shui*, which is female energy or *yin,* represented in water; and *shan*, which is male energy or *yang,* represented in mountain-heaven. The artist achieves universal harmony in balancing the yin and the yang. Balance is further achieved in the ancient art of calligraphy. Calligraphy to the Chinese is an art form that intimately relates to other art forms. Both calligraphy and poetry are elements of accomplished Chinese landscape paintings. Calligraphy is also the written vehicle of poetry. In a Chinese painting, lines of poetry add an important visual element that contributes to the aesthetic aspects of the painting and provides a poetic commentary. Poets become calligraphers and, as such, artists, demonstrating the strong interconnections of the "three perfections": calligraphy, poetry, and art. Insofar as the Chinese often call painting "silent poetry," in order to become a painter the artist first had to understand the philosophy inherent in poetry. It was equally important to have mastered the calligraphic brush-strokes.[6] Without an understanding of these interconnections, an outsider is limited to an emic appreciation of Chinese art.

What the primacy of space in Chinese art implies for the understanding of its aesthetics and meaning is not accessible to an outsider unfamiliar with the traditional Chinese interpretation of space. The aesthetics of space unique to this art imbue concepts of universal balance and harmony with the energies accorded male and female—the yin and yang principles. Space relates to the entire composition, defining the organization or placement of the content elements, as well as the interaction of each of the formal elements within the confines of the work. Chinese artists use multiple perspectives, also called shifting perspectives, to create illusions of space, typical of a mindset that approaches an issue or a visual statement from multiple points of view. Their ethics of polytheism, which allow for various approaches to the concept of reality, is affirmed in their application of multiple perspectives in art.

This is very different from the Western Renaissance artists, who were committed to using the one-point perspective. Renaissance art is an excellent example of how art echoes the ethics of a culture as visual manifestations of its time. Christianity is monotheistic; its attitude of absolutism, together with its mono-causal approach to right or wrong, was translated in art into the one-point perspective.

On the one hand, any viewer can appreciate the beauty of Islamic architecture, for which Islamic art is best known in the West; the traditionally illustrated manuscripts, on the other hand, are less accessible to outsiders. In the sumptuous, colorful narrations illustrating the history of Islamic rulers, their battles, and glorious courts, artists were honoring the notion that only Allah could create. Unlike Indian art, no representation of Mohammad or Allah was permitted. Conventions forbade realistic or life-like representations of people and their faces. The result was the standardized representations of humans as two-dimensional stick figures. Rather than depicting a particular individual, figures are cast as type-forms, serving as examples or symbols of humans with minimal individuation or distinction between males and females, with the exception of clothing and facial hair. True to the general Islamic view of women's role in society, women were without exception marginalized and depicted in the art in lesser detail and smaller size compared to male figures, and usually placed in the periphery. These illustrations also reveal the Islamic concept that, no matter which gender, the individual is less important per se than the group or community.

The above examples culled from three different cultures demonstrate that, even if we only aspire to gain a subjective appreciation of a work and limit ourselves to viewing the emic aspects, without a working knowledge of the concepts that lie behind the aesthetic, we need to do our homework on the culture in question to do justice to its complexity. Without this knowledge we're unable to perceive the works as the Indians, Chinese, or Muslims do.

A viewer, unfamiliar with the cultural values and subject matters often referenced in indigenous myths and legends, is unable to access the richness of what is being communicated. A recontextualization automatically takes place when art is moved from its original context to a new cultural setting. Since the function for which it was created is no longer relevant or understood, its original meaning is invalidated.

New owners of works of art often lack interest and knowledge of the original context. Examples are sculptures and ivories from the last decade of 19th-century West Africa. Over 2,400 Benin objects were brought from Africa and placed in various museums and private collections. These objects, which signified hierarchical powers, were originally mostly created to be used in rituals. A layman who encounters works of art from an unfamiliar culture will immediately go to its lowest common denominator, which is its subject matter. Western viewers recontextualized Benin art for their own purpose, since they were unable to appreciate it from the perspective of its intended function. Their response was to ignore African symbolic (iconographic) meanings (iconologic) by recontextualizing it to serve in the new context, as merely exotic, decorative conversation pieces.

Biases are inherent in cross-cultural spectatorship and are not unique to Western viewers. The built-in bias inherent in every act of recontextualization works both ways. Artists, too, recontextualize, as exemplified in the artistic borrowings particularly prevalent in postmodern art, as we'll discuss in more detail in chapter 5. The painting *I Don't Want to Play Cards with Cezanne,* by Chinese artist Li Chao, exemplifies an artist's conscious cross-cultural recontextualization. Li Chao based his work on a reinterpretation of Cézanne's 1915 painting, *Card Players,* both in terms of composition and style. In the words of art historian Richard E. Strassberg, "Li Chao's painting embodies this contradiction by appropriating and simultaneously rejecting an image by Cézanne."[7] Li Chao offers a new interpretation by articulating his own interpretation through the language of art. In general, many contemporary non-Western artists have no access to original modern Western art, but study these from reproductions in books and magazines. Caught in the struggle of trying to understand their own traditions, as well as learning about those of Western art, they're faced with the challenge to enter into the artistic domain of the freedom of expression offered by modern art without losing their cultural identity. In acknowledging art as universal property, artists recontextualize it, using the art as subject matter. *I Don't Want to Play Cards with Cezanne* is just one example of artists' conscious cross-cultural recontextualization.

In a lecture I presented at the Beijing Academy of Fine Arts, I focused on a selected number of American artists. The work of Martin Green particularly puzzled the students. Their comments were appreciative, but also quite critical. They felt the artist had misunderstood the correct Chinese perspective in rendering a mountainscape. While it's true that Green was inspired by Chinese landscape painting, his work was not intended to be a statement on Chinese art. On the other hand, when the students saw Grant Wood's *American Gothic,* depicting the farm couple posing in front of their barn with pitchfork in hand, they immediately identified with the painting's strong statements of stoicism and work ethic.

Unconsciously, viewers see art through the filter of their respective culture's aesthetics. The two examples cited above illustrate that, whether a Chinese painter uses Western art as his point of departure, or an American artist uses Chinese art as his inspiration, accepting recontextualized art on the same basis as the ethnic art that inspired it can be problematic. The viewer's immediate response to these works is to criticize them for being imitative and failing to measure up to the viewer's assumptions regarding the painter's intent. Viewed as ethnic art, recontextualized works elicit either outright dismissal, or are judged harshly according to the benchmarks of the so-called authentic ethnic art.

Take for example a Chinese artist who paints a landscape first in the traditional Chinese style, then another in a Western style. The two works, though painted by the same artist, are judged by different standards, and often the Western-style painting is seen as less authentic. Lucy Lippard points out that when Western artists show cross-cultural influences from Asian art, they're praised as innovative, and their art is heralded as original. Yet, when minority artists emulate aspects of Western art, they're criticized for it, and their art is dismissed as derivative.[8]

Most viewers automatically look at works of art from other cultures through the filter of their own aesthetic conditioning. Some art is relatively easy to place in its original context by determining where it belongs in the modernization continuum. When we've identified where the object under examination belongs on the tradition-modernity scale, we've made an important first step. Once the historic context of a work of art is determined, we'll know what to expect and will be better equipped to recognize the contribution of the artist in relation to whether he or she confirms or reforms the cultural tradition of his time.

Historically, different cultures have nurtured their artists either by public or private support. A prominent example of government-sponsored art is the Chinese politicized art during the reign of Chairman Mao, founder of the Communist Party of China and the People's Republic of China. Under the threat of persecution, artists were forced to follow Mao's agenda as expressed in his 1942 *Talks at the Yan'an Forum on Literature and Art.* Art was first and foremost to be produced in the service of the revolution; any other artistic concerns were secondary. The slogan "art for the people by the people and about the people" held Chinese self-expression in art captive well past Mao's death in 1976. Typically, artists were to display happy workers on the farms or in the factories, in the social-realism style that originated in the Soviet Union.

In a similar way and closer to home, minority and third-world artists, when reviewed by Western critics, weren't until recently accorded the freedom to choose to be an artist first, and only then an individual of a certain ethnicity or persuasion. Their artistic ability was critiqued according to one of three criteria: primarily, they were expected to work in a given technique, style, and subject matter, while re-creating values of the traditional art of their cultural past; second, they might apply Western techniques and styles to non-culture-specific subject matters; the third alternative was to draw upon elements culled from their indigenous folk art and create sometimes highly abstract renderings of modernized semi-abstract imagery. By failing to apply consistent critical criteria, reviewers continue to drive a wedge between certain artists and their art.

Over the last few decades, artists have slowly freed themselves from the bondage of their respective traditions, and in the spirit of Postmodernism, culled ideas and techniques from around the world. Part of their agenda is not only to free themselves from the bondage of tradition, but also to have the freedom to retain, expand, or change elements of that tradition, or to borrow from the visual traditions of any other time or culture.

A viewer should consider this information in accordance with the conventions and styles of the art of the culture under investigation. Viewers know that understanding and interpretation of a work of art go beyond looking. Seeing involves a step-by-step process that may seem cumbersome to an inexperienced viewer, but with experience can become second nature.

A change in attitude allows us to broaden our horizon, but this hinges on gathering information and developing a code of values that can align our presuppositions with an interpretation appropriate to the given context. Whenever we analyze feelings, we'll meet challenges. It takes courage to learn to accept what we don't understand. Though we keep probing for meanings in a work of art, the meanings remain indeterminate. Yet in spite of this, we can appreciate the art as we let go of our need of absolute answers in our encounters with dimensions that reach beyond our comprehension.

In the following chapter, we'll see that the same dynamics apply as we learn how to decode people. Each interpretation is contingent on the particular perspective we use. If we want to go beyond a superficial level of understanding either art or people, we must be aware that understanding unfolds as a process. In the words of da Vinci, "You should approach a work of art as if you are approaching a majesty, a king." We should approach people in the same way we approach art. An individual's appearance is largely self-created; therefore, an individual is as much an artistic statement as a work of art is. As the saying goes, art imitates life, and life imitates art.

3

Decoding People

People are works of art in process. We don't always have to like what we see, but we can't be satisfied leaving the encounter on the level of likes or dislikes. It's important to understand why we respond as we do, and to explore the underlying reasons and the effects our responses have on us.

George Bernard Shaw suggested that when we don't like someone, it's because we don't know him or her well enough. Or does familiarity breed contempt, as another familiar adage suggests? Perhaps our contempt is occasioned simply by a reflection of certain dubious qualities in ourselves that we may not want to acknowledge. Either way, encounters with others give us an opportunity for self-discovery that could lead to a deeper acceptance of ourselves. To our own surprise, we may find that the contempt engendered in the first encounter is no longer present in subsequent encounters. Acceptance of our own weaknesses allows for the same in others.

We often hear the expression that someone can be read "like an open book." While reading a child is comparatively easy, a grown person poses a different challenge. No matter how beautiful the book cover, it doesn't necessarily reflect the quality of its content. Appearances can be deceiving.

Encountering a stranger requires emotional and social intelligence; we must know ourselves before we can aspire to know another. A person is always more than meets the eye. It's only fair to assume that another human being is as interesting and complex as we consider ourselves to be. We show respect not only because we realize that respect begets respect, but also because we've heightened our awareness. We'll acknowledge that when we meet another person, we're indeed meeting a self who perceives us as an "other." Keep in mind that to go half-way is an invitation to dare bridge the perceived gap.

In this chapter we propose a viewing process for decoding people only slightly modified from the process we use to decode art. By practicing observing facial features, body language, and attire, and making every visual clue count, we can gain fundamental insights about that person. We must go at it with a neutral yet inquisitive attitude, however, sensitive to the fact that we and the person we meet are products of culturally conditioned circumstances that affect perceptual habits, as well as the visual statement that we make in our respective manners and appearance.

Though every individual is well worth getting to know, we obviously spend more time with those who interest us the most. This is a conscious decision, based on the same way we look at a work of art—by asking questions directly or engaging in our own inner dialogue. Since many of us are innately shy and reluctant to reveal personal information, we can encourage conversation by volunteering information about ourselves first. After gaining the trust of the other, we gather basic data including occupation, and by inference, general economic status. While we talk, we observe visual details of his or her appearance; these, together with previous experiences, help us put together a sketch that makes an otherwise stereotypic profile fade. Even as we're listening and verbally exchanging information, we make assessments through independent visual observation. We draw upon our memory bank, recognizing in the new person a composite of people we've already come to know.

Regarding First Impressions

A first impression is made in a few fleeting seconds. The way we present ourselves determines how others see us. We can manipulate that first impression to our own advantage, which raises two important questions. Do we see ourselves as others see us? Do others see themselves as we see them?

Whether consciously or not, both the observer and the observed are image makers; it works both ways, for each is a visual statement—just like art. Our clothes and cosmetics are the paint, and our bodies are the canvas. These canvases are what we offer people to view, inviting them to form their own interpretations. But very few among us know which clues to look for. If we're inexperienced in decoding the messages inherent in an appearance, we may not see any more in others than they choose to reveal.

We should consider a first impression as a temporary stepping-stone. Getting to know a person better and perhaps finding our first impression inaccurate won't happen if we can't get past that first impression. To acknowledge that a person isn't who we originally pegged them to be, and to recognize that our perceptions were clouded by the prejudice of unconsciously held assumptions, is a rare quality we all should strive for. Only by drawing on considerable experience can we walk away from a first encounter with someone feeling that we know the person. We also need to keep in mind that our personal experiences don't constitute universal truths—these, too, are subject to a reality check. Each person is at least as unique as we consider ourselves to be.

In decoding people or art, we move from the general characteristics to the specific by registering the immediate visual impressions, while considering gender, age, and the context of time and place, in anticipation of later interpretation. To what extent should we trust our first impression? Here we need to proceed with caution. As John C. Condon and Mitsuko Saito remind us, "When a person hears words in a language he has never studied, he not only does not understand the words, he knows that he is not understanding." Yet we don't always achieve this level of consciousness with nonverbal communications, which "a person can completely misunderstand without ever realizing that he has misunderstood."[1]

During a first encounter, we put out feelers and form an intuitive impression. Inevitably we profile or stereotype, categorizing new experiences based on the old. Recognizing the limitations inherent in first encounters is a key aspect of visual literacy—a commitment to remain open-minded as we internalize our awareness and monitor our attitudes.

Learning to listen without interrupting is an expression of politeness, universally accepted as part of civilized society. Learning to listen with ears and eyes, and observing other people's listening skills, also gives us information about their genuine or assumed interest in us. Voices are very telling as we gather clues. When people engage in small talk, they speak volumes about themselves: vocabulary, intonation, and modulation are all indicators of who they are.

The situations and circumstances that allow for face-to-face encounters will, of course, determine the quality of these experiences. Consider the difference between a personal and a professional meeting. In both cases, just as we experienced with art, the context of time and place is significant. For example, compare the differences in your own behavior—

how you act, talk, and dress—when you're at work, out shopping, or at home. Most of us probably realize that our demeanor changes with our circumstances. We bring a specific *self* to the forefront, depending on whom we're with. The trick is to recognize the mannerisms and specific conducts that signify and separate our private self from our public self—which self do we present when we meet a stranger?

When we find ourselves in first encounters in a multicultural situation, we need to be aware of culture-specific etiquettes. This pertains specifically to the behavior of gendered company. In several cultures there are marked distinctions between how men are expected to conduct themselves while relating to women, and vice versa. Another cultural difference to pay attention to are attitudes regarding the elderly. Particularly in Eastern cultures, age is treated with utmost respect.[2]

Skillfully observing other people reveals information about their self-image, level of confidence, and social standing, precisely the knowledge we seek. Even as we verbally exchange information with someone, we simultaneously pass visual judgment, looking for harmony between what we see and what we hear. Keep in mind that our own behavior also colors the impressions we give.

Reading Face and Body Language

It's evident that almost all human characteristics have both universal and culture-specific aspects. Artists assume that a person's face best reveals the character of its bearer and therefore pay the most attention to the face. From infancy we recognize emotions through observing facial expression. Though emotions are universal, how each of them is expressed is culture-specific. People have an entire spectrum of feelings, from hunger and fear to love and compassion; however, their manifestations aren't universally identical. In certain East Asian cultures it's considered ill-mannered to express emotions. Children are educated to control themselves to the extent that their faces remain expressionless. This can be bewildering for Westerners.

We generally regard the eyes in particular as the most telling part of a person. As windows to the soul, eyes are most expressive. They don't lie. This is why, for instance, a person who's guilty of a crime, but unpracticed in deception, won't look another straight in the eyes. But avoiding eye contact can also be culturally conditioned. The habit of looking into someone's eyes when either speaking or being spoken to, which Westerners consider polite and take for granted as an important aspect in reading an individual's character, is by no means universal—it depends on culturally conditioned etiquette. In many cultures, a woman avoids eye contact by averting her eyes from a man's gaze. If she were to exchange glances, it would be interpreted as an invitation. In Japan, for example, it's common to avoid eye contact, no matter the gender; even in a job interview, the interviewer won't look into the eyes of the interviewee.

A facial expression that has different connotations in various cultures is the smile. In the United States smiling is considered polite, and we're expected to smile when we meet another person, whether we like them or not. Sincere or not, the smile conveys a degree of happiness or satisfaction, or at the very least an absence of ill will. Even alluring smiles are polite in American culture, and girls are trained to use their smiles advantageously. We're all familiar with images of young and sexy women with broad, toothy smiles, eye candy in ads, bidding us to purchase a whole spectrum of products we didn't know we needed. On the other hand, a Korean student once explained in class that in professional situations in her country, if a woman smiled at a strange man, he'd think she was a prostitute. Declining to smile is neither intended as rudeness nor seen as arrogance—Korean women are simply trained not to smile in certain social situations.

But smiling or not isn't always a culturally specific behavior; it could simply be an expression of a personal situation. Some people instinctively cover their mouths when they smile, which could be nothing more than a gesture to conceal bad teeth or bad breath.

Cosmetics remake faces, accentuating or camouflaging features, allowing us to alter the image we want to project. Using cosmetics to conform to societal standards of beauty shields the users from being easily read. This is much like an artist using numerical rather than descriptive labels as identifiers for his or her work, leaving the viewer with one less clue to understand the artist's intent.

If artists consider the face the most significant expression of a person's personality and character, hands run a close second. Men with elongated fingers and well-manicured nails are considered feminine;

women with the same are seen as elevated in the class structure, if not also somewhat proud and vain. Bitten, rough, uncared-for nails suggest the opposite, no matter the gender. Hands, unlike a person's face, cannot lie about their age.

If the face is our canvas, the body is its extension, and the viewer expects to find consistency between the two. One area of consistency that the viewer considers is body language. Gestures supplement verbal communications and are also part of a person's ethnic and cultural heritage. Such gestures are so deeply ingrained that we use them unconsciously. Their symbolic meanings vary from culture to culture and are not always readily accessible to an outsider.

Inappropriate responses to unfamiliar body language can cause misunderstandings and hinder interpersonal communication between people of various cultures. For example, American men like to display feelings of friendship for one another with a slap on the back or, in the case of athletes, on the backside. In some Asian countries this would be totally unacceptable! Finding two American males walking hand-in-hand would likely indicate a sexual relationship between the two, but in some Asian countries this gesture indicates nothing more than a close platonic friendship. People from countries in Southern Europe greet each other with hugs and kisses on either cheek, with very little regard for gender or age. Yet in East Asian cultures, where people greet each other by bowing, this type of bodily contact would be considered rude. Americans often greet one another with a handshake, and shaking hands is also becoming commonplace in Asia, especially in the business community. While this gesture is a sign of good will, lack of eye contact coupled with a limp handshake leaves a Westerner with the impression of the person as weak, indecisive, and untrustworthy.

It's important to be aware of the nonverbal components of communication and to be sensitive to the dangers of our natural tendencies to shape others in our own image. One of the most obvious nonverbal components we display are the clothes we choose to wear. Our bodies house our essence, but our clothes cover our bodies.

Interpreting Dress and Style

One's initial impression of a person frequently elicits a spontaneous emotional response. We begin visually by studying a person in totality—face, body, and dress—all at once.

Whereas we readily understand that clothes do more than satisfy climatic needs, we observe the clothes as we would a book cover, expecting the jacket to hint at the content. Whether we dress for ourselves or for how we wish to be perceived by others, clothes send messages about us, about our personality and our confidence. In most cases they reveal not only the economic status of the wearer, but also sociopolitical inclinations and degrees of conformity.

We make a statement with the clothes we choose to wear, often accentuating it with accessories, jewelry, and cosmetics. We go about presenting ourselves with the creative effort of an artist preparing for an exhibition. We are our own canvases.

A person's clothing has the same function as a caption to a painting. Clothes give an observer a direction that can define, disguise, or obscure who we are. Our facial expressions invite interpretation, and our clothes are an extension of that interpretation, reflecting how we adjust to specific contexts, situations, times, and places. Some blindly follow fashion, while others try to create an image that reflects who they are or wish to become. Still others, short on cash or self-confidence, choose clothes that make them blend in with their surroundings. Unfortunately there's no guarantee that people will see us how we'd like to be seen or interpret our dress as we intend them to.

Clothing, like cosmetics, can be perceived as human packaging. If the packaging looks good, then we assume its contents are good. Minimally, people's clothing reveals their social status. The way we dress affects how others perceive and interact with us, for better or worse, as illustrated in an incident related by a student:

> A group of friends were at Denny's. We agreed that we should each pay separately. When the bill came, my friend, a white male, had no problem paying his portion by credit card. No identification was asked for. But when our Mexican friend was paying, the waitress asked for his ID.

Now pay close attention to what follows:

> I found this so appalling that, because of his being Mexican, there was some type of assumption that he could not have an authentic credit card. In fact, what was so upsetting is that he was wearing the nicest shirt (a polo shirt) and was clean-shaven.

The student probably didn't realize that she, too, exhibited a nascent form of racism in her expectation that her friend's kempt attire should have been viewed as exceptional for his ethnicity.

Of course, manner of dress isn't the only culturally conditioned aspect of clothing; the degree of dress is a further consideration. Different cultures see nudity within a spectrum ranging from acceptance to shame. In Scandinavia public nudity is not a sexual statement, but an expression of a respect for the natural beauty of the unclothed body. There, women's freedom to sunbathe and swim bare-breasted also expresses equality, since men only cover the lower part of their bodies. From this we can see that the degree and state of dress is culturally conditioned. On the other hand, we see sexual statements in the very notion of what clothing covers. Fishnet stockings, for example, intend to draw attention not to what we can see, but to what we can't. As with cleavage-revealing tops, fishnet stockings are suggestive of what we don't see. The idiom "dressed to kill" says it all.

In the past, women had to suffer for beauty, in the East as well as the West; witness Chinese foot-binding and Euro-American corsets. High-heeled shoes, giving women additional height and stature, are a contemporary example. Even today, in spite of confirmed, long-term physical harm, high heels are worn as a symbol of high fashion and femininity, especially in cosmopolitan centers. As Forrest Gump wisely noted, "Momma always says there's an awful lot you could tell about a person by their shoes."

Today, as always, availability, economy, and taste determine what people wear. This is also the case in the USA, even though the country imports 96 percent of its clothing. Before production, manufacturers conduct market analyses in the target country based on tastes and buying habits. In the end, the fact that what a person wears comes from a multicultural marketplace doesn't mean that the multicultural marketplace fashions the styles that Americans wear. Americans themselves are multicultural, and their culturally specific taste in clothing clearly influences the fashions and styles produced in the multicultural marketplace.

The freedom to choose the way they dress reflects the degree of freedom people have in any society at any given time. Even today, the freedom to choose is dictated by the occasion. One type of clothing is worn to work, be it sitting at a desk or doing manual labor, and another to religious ceremonies, and yet others to festivals and recreational events. The aesthetics match the functions.

We encounter uniformed people on a daily basis: soldiers in khakis, doctors in white smocks, nurses in green scrubs, police in blue polyester, or prisoners in orange jumpers. All of these uniforms identify the wearers as members of a collective rather than as individuals. In America as well as in other countries, uniforms are required in some K-12 public and private schools. The primary reason is to alleviate economic pressures on those financially challenged, thereby discouraging competition or one-upmanship, and encouraging equality. Another argument for school uniforms is that they eliminate social and religious differences, promoting social integration. Banning students from wearing religious attire to school goes against the grain of Muslims, however, who have their own dress code and perceive school dress codes as a governmental policy of secularizing Islam. Muslim fathers and husbands insist on the right of their wives and daughters to wear veils or headscarves as a symbol of their moral submission to Islam. This has led to misunderstandings and heated debates caused by a lack of mutual respect for cultural differences.

An opposing tendency is to dress as a nonconformist, yet in doing so the individual often conforms to the nonconformists. Shocking hairstyles, body piercings, tattoos, and edgy clothes confirm membership in a counterculture, at least until the styles are appropriated by the popular culture.

And now, a cautionary note: Whether sizing up a conformist in a suit or a nonconformist in low-riders, a young man in coveralls or a young woman in a skimpy party dress, we must take care in assessing a person based on appearance. Viewing a person simply as an object is dehumanizing and misleading. Our purpose in developing visual literacy is to learn to analyze with context in mind before we make any inferences, recognizing that the primary context for people or art is, indeed, culture.

Recognizing Gender Specificities

Up to this point we've discussed factors that influence our first impressions of people we encounter, such as facial expression, body language, and manner of dress. In a sense, these are the emic aspects of the work of art—the person—under our perusal. Now we'll consider the etic perspective: the person in the broader cultural context of place and time—the type of information supplied in a museum label.

From the beginning of time, men and women have been delegated specific gender-based roles. These roles are still defined in reference to both physical and psychological differences. Men and women approach and see reality from different perspectives, based on biological as well as socio-cultural and environmental conditions, though which is the largest contributor to these difference is still in dispute. One factor not in dispute is that first impressions hinge largely on gender.

Traditionally, gender distinction tends to subordinate women's roles to those of men. Women in many cultures are defined according to their relation to men and in terms of the place they hold in the family. A woman is a daughter of, sister of, wife of, mother of, and so on. In the past, gender roles in the world at large, and in certain countries today, show preference for male children. In some countries, having a daughter means paying hefty dowries. Parents want a son, particularly in Asian cultures, where women can't officiate at burial rites for religious reasons. Another asset sons hold is their ability to continue the family name.

In traditional cultures, segregation of sexes begins at an early age and continues throughout life. Some mosques and synagogues post signs forbidding women who are menstruating from entering to prevent them from defiling sacred spaces, and in most, women are separated from men and relegated to specific areas in the back, the balcony, or behind screens, and are kept at a distance from the religious sermon. Bias against women is also expressed in most major religious texts. In many cases, discriminatory interpretations were added to texts and subsequently institutionalized. Some of these are more explicit than others, such as the Hadith's Koranic commentaries or the Hindu scriptures. Occasionally however, God has thrown women a bone, as in this delightful quote from the Talmud:

> Be very careful if you make a woman cry, because God counts her tears. The woman came out of a man's rib. Not from his feet to be walked on. Not from his head to be superior, but from the side to be equal. Under the arm to be protected, and next to the heart to be loved.

A woman in patriarchal societies has few choices; she can marry, bare children, become a caregiver, a nun, or a prostitute. In modern urban spaces, this tradition has been largely breached, mostly where the high cost of living has made dual incomes a necessity for an affluent lifestyle. Since the 1970s, feminists have become increasingly active in addressing the perception of women as second-class citizens. Women have gained emancipation in certain fields and have been instrumental in effecting positive change.

Women are increasingly seeking education in order to pursue careers and fulfill their own ambitions, in part to contribute economically to the family unit, and also to actively participate in the education of their children. Even so, a woman's obligations outside of the home often fail to result in equal sharing of household chores between husband and wife—more often than not, the wife shoulders the majority of mundane household responsibilities in addition to her career and child-rearing duties.

Feminists have shed light on inequities related to sexism that still dominate governmental institutions and fiscal policy-making decisions; nevertheless, either overt or covert gender discrimination follows a female throughout her life, as well as an underevaluation as a separate, independent individual.

Women's ongoing assent to their subordinate roles can be measured in their tone of voice, which typically conveys a tentative rather than authoritative tone. Actor Dustin Hoffman remarked that his biggest challenge in preparing to play the role of a woman in the 1982 film *Tootsie* was to end his female character's lines with a rising inflection, as if they were questions. Such a manner of intonation suggests that women are wont to speak with trepidation, perhaps fearing that a tone expressing too much authority would somehow compromise their femininity.

Worldwide, gender discrimination is apparent in sports, education, business, and many other aspects of daily living. Less acknowledged is language discrimination, still apparent in most cultures. One example in English is the *Mr.* title for males and *Mrs.* for married females, revealing an unconscious acceptance of male dominance. In filling out forms, women are asked to choose between *Miss, Mrs.*, or *Ms.*, the latter serving as a counterpoint to *Mr.*, a neutral marker of marital status. The male is acknowledged *de facto* as a man; however, a woman is acknowledged traditionally in relation to her marital status. As another example, in the USA it has been the assumption, until relatively recently, that a woman will assume her husband's last name upon marriage. She now has the option of retaining her maiden name, and some opt for a hyphenated name. The man, however, is not expected to take on his spouse's name, as demonstrated in a recent lawsuit in which the American Civil Liberties Union (ACLU) advocated for a California man's equal protection under the 14th Amendment to change his surname upon marriage to that of his spouse.[3]

Discrimination is similarly imbedded in the gender-specific nomenclature identifying certain professions that women only lately have had access to. Policemen are now known as police officers, firemen as firefighters; mailmen are now postal carriers, and chairmen have become chairpersons. Many people are still unaware of the discriminatory implications of their colloquial language and use the masculine third-person pronoun "he" as a generic pronoun for both sexes. Many still use the term *forefathers*, because who talks about *foremothers*? Feminist contributions to linguistic reform insist that the correct and gender-free term is *forebears*. Similarly, if feminists have their say, the term *humankind* will one day supplant *mankind* as a term more symbolically inclusive of women as well as their male counterparts.

Creating Self-Images and Cultural Identities

Remember the impact of first impressions, the suggestive power of appearance? All we needed was a few moments to assess someone, based on his or her outward appearance and mannerisms, without even meaning to. In this brief time we gathered clues to the person's past, present, and future. We began visually by studying the person in totality—face, body, and dress—all at once.

But getting beyond this first encounter without deluding ourselves and misjudging the other requires interpretation that takes the other's personal choices regarding face, body, and dress into a deeper consideration of his or her cultural context.

What predisposes us to judge another person's looks—even our own—on a scale of 1-10? In Western society, standards of beauty are articulated through persistent advertisements. The message is, if you're too fat or otherwise imperfect, according to standards agreed upon by society, help is out there. Endless infomercials get the message across. Beauty builds self-esteem! Looks matter! There are dietary plans you can subscribe to and miracle exercise equipment you can buy! If you don't have the time, patience, or self-discipline, you can try pills, liposuction, gastric bypass surgery—any number of medical interventions are available![4]

Of course, medical intervention is controversial. Though the social stigma against it is waning, health risks remain. In spite of this, parents who share their daughter's dissatisfaction with her looks are sympathetic and supportive. Girls are easily seduced at an ever-younger age by the omnipresent imagery of glamorous media stars, little realizing that their heroes are themselves addicted to the perfect female ideal. With so many procedures available—breast augmentation, lip enhancement, nose jobs, and more—elective surgery seems no different from putting on makeup.

All the hype over outer beauty tends to overlook the value of inner beauty. What constitutes beauty is a question of taste and, more explicitly, a question of cultural conditioning. What is seen as beauty in one culture is not necessarily so in another, although Western criteria for beauty, pushed by media images, are so pervasive that women throughout the world have embraced these ideals, as reflected in the popularity of Miss Universe contests.[5]

Today's preoccupation with the perfect image, as magnified by Hollywood, is symptomatic of the worship of youthful beauty, leaving the intrinsic worth of the aging population in dire neglect. Of course, interest in manipulating natural signs of aging is nothing new. Still, convention has it that aging men are more attractive than aging women. We tend to describe older gentlemen as "distinguished," but aging women are simply "old."

Older women are especially sensitive to the requirements of beauty maintenance. Some of us recall white hair—tinted lightly in either soft pink or baby blue—and too-heavily powdered faces with thin, painted lips and sharply delineated eyebrows, so common among older women in the late 20th century. They dressed for town, ready to be seen, yet looked just like any other. It required a large investment of both time and money to perpetuate the façade that made it difficult for the observer to penetrate. The pink and blue hair of older women have gone by the wayside only to be replaced by updated fashion trends, but the intent to conform to beauty standards in order to stand out remains the same.

Of course, our attitudes toward aging are irrational to say the least, considering the inevitability of the aging process. Children yearn to be older, but when they reach a certain age, adults long for their youth. For example, a teenager would say, "I'm 13 going on 14," or "I'm 13-and-a-half." But who says, "I'm 35-and-a-half?" Women past 45 avoid telling their age altogether, although centenarians proudly state theirs. Some people wear their wrinkles with pride, while others use cosmetics to conceal the inevitable, giving rise to exponential growth in the cosmetics industry. Cosmetic companies target women as prime candidates for their products. This obsession with youth is not yet as prevalent in developing countries as it is in the USA, though in the near future we can expect to see a shift in those cultures as well.

Cosmetics are a double-edge sword: on the one hand they allow the user to slide into the current standards of beauty set by society, yet on the other hand the user is in danger of losing the unique characteristics that define her. This in turn results in perpetuating stereotypes.

Disguising signs of aging through cosmetic, surgical, or other interventions clearly misses the point of honoring visible aspects of natural maturation and growth. Some see the eradication of signs of aging as minimizing an individual's life experience and warping the celebration of longevity. It's interesting to note that people who strive to hide their age reveal a great deal about themselves and their manner of coping with life, as do those who allow nature to take its course. Wrinkles are indeed the footprints of time.

Knowing a person's age is not unessential—it's all part of the decoding process. As we strive for visual literacy we'll learn to look past our expectations, as well as those of the other self who wears the face, and see beyond what it might otherwise keep to itself.

As we've discussed, the way we dress, be it dressy or casual, formal or informal, speaks volumes. Shabby is to dress, as graffiti is to fine art, or slang to Standard English. In addition to the immediate visual clues, we combine our collected data and formulate our understanding of the persons we want to know.

In Asia, traditional national costumes are gaining popularity and are being worn to most formal occasions. Looking closer at the attire, we realize that certain moral values are vested in them. The clothing reveals attitudes regarding a woman's place in the context of family.

Take for instance the Vietnamese wardrobe. Responding to modern fashions, the traditionally full-length *ao dai*, a dress-like tunic, has become shorter and shorter, and now falls just below the knees. Young girls are expected to wear only pastel-colored or white garments, while married women wear either dark or bright tunics over black or white pants, though today these color codes are not as stringently observed.

The Indian sari and the Japanese kimono have undergone a similar development, advancing from entirely modest designs to designs more freely emphasizing the female figure. In examining their respective styles, we can learn to what degree their traditions have modernized. Many would hold that such changes have come about through Westernization, since frequently Westernization is equated with modernization.

In the Soviet Union and in China during Mao's reign, dress codes were imposed as symbolic of both political sovereignty and cultural conformity. The so-called Mao uniform exemplifies part of that ideology, consisting of a cap, a jacket with a mandarin collar, and pants all in the same color, with virtually no difference between male and female clothing design. Women and girls were not permitted to wear jewelry or cosmetics, and their hair was worn in either one or two braids. Clothing is a great equalizer, the reason behind many uniform policies. When we dress the same way, we experience a sense of equality and communal identity.

Aspects of the visual culture of a nation demonstrate how individuals are representative of their culture. This is beautifully illustrated on a commemorative stamp of Gandhi's official visit to Buckingham

Palace in 1939. Gandhi, the father of India's independence, was true to his political ethic of frugality when he wore the simple, hand-spun *dothi*, the counterpart of the *sari* worn by women. Gandhi's dothi symbolized his policies of self-reliance during the struggle for independence.

There's no escaping context. Context seen from any perspective is always cultural. Artists function from within their cultural or multicultural contexts, as do viewers. On the macro level, governments are likewise concerned with the image they present to the public and the world. This is clearly reflected not only in national dress, but also in national iconography inherent in such items as flags, money, and stamps. These function as national unifiers and are manifestations of culture-specific properties, creating a sense of unity and separate identity, the symbolic meanings being inaccessible to those on the outside. You might be carrying an excellent example of an object rich in cultural symbolism right now in your purse or wallet—try out the "Dollar Bill Speaks" experiment in appendix A on page 131.

As with so many human qualities, those that define virtue are culture-specific. In Japanese culture, modesty is one such quality that has visual as well as other manifestations. It implies humility and requires a soft-spoken voice and modest attire. It also requires a fair amount of sensitivity and cultural literacy in order to accommodate the harmonious coexistence that this built-in social mechanism affords. Takao Suzuki describes Japanese society as "a society in which the common practice is to try to guess others' feelings and wishes before they are verbally expressed. This also explains why the Japanese themselves call their culture *sasshi no bunka*, literally, 'guessing culture'; and *omoiyari no bunk*, 'consideration culture.'"[6]

Because it's deemed essential to identify with the other and feel as he or she feels, a free exchange of opposing views between individuals in Japanese society is restrained to the utmost. Non-Japanese may falsely interpret the reluctance to engage in confrontations as a character flaw, rather than a culturally conditioned ethic stipulating conformity as a virtue and limiting individual expression to the confines of the family. An old Japanese proverb addresses this quite succinctly: "the nail that sticks up the most will receive the most pounding. In stark contrast Americans say, "The squeaky wheel gets the grease," encouraging them to stand up for their rights and assert themselves lest they be ignored.

Tone of voice is instrumental in decoding the giving and receiving of compliments, but it's only one a piece of the puzzle. The etiquette of giving compliments within a culture and cross-culturally, who gives them and to whom, in which situations, and how they're received are equally essential in the decoding process. In the USA compliments are received with a simple "thank you" or "you're so kind," acknowledging the generous intent of the complimenter. Compliments there can also function as indicators of social standing. In many countries in Asia and Europe compliments are received with a denial, with the intent of deflecting the compliment. If for example you're told that you've cooked a fabulous meal, the proper response would be, "Oh no, it is nothing. I am sorry I offered you such poor fare," thereby putting yourself beneath the complimenter and thus elevating his or her social standing. Compliments therefore are not necessarily indicative of reality—they may often be greatly exaggerated, but are nonetheless offered in the same hospitable spirit as a meal.

In the following chapter we'll explore culture as experienced by an individual, as well as seen as a collective process. At each stage a culture is subject to redefinitions provided by changing sociopolitical contexts.

PART II
CULTURAL LITERACY

4

Processing and Decoding Cultures

Our journey in this text, to better understand ourselves, others, and the cultures we belong to, started out with our individual perceptions of art and culture. In decoding art, we come to appreciate the interplay between the artist and the culture that produced the art. Through this experience we prepare ourselves to formulate appropriate questions to understand the art and culture of others.

We begin this chapter by defining culture in its many facets. Culture supplies the context for who we are and how we define our self-identity. Awareness of the cultural contexts of art and of people facilitates our understanding of both. Just as the heart can't be separated from the mind, neither can art be separated from culture. The question of what culture is has no simple answer. In a general way we conceive nature and culture as reality, yet our conception of nature and culture is an amalgamation of individually and collectively learned responses to our environment, communicated through individually and collectively learned modes of communication.

Three key concepts that define a culture are ethos, ethics, and aesthetics. These concepts fuse as they interact with each other. Together they function as a partial platform for exploring and interpreting visual statements. The interaction between these concepts is central to any culture:

- Ethos is the complex umbrella concept that applies to the distinctive character or characteristics of a culture. A construct operating on a theoretical level, ethos represents the attitudes, beliefs, and mental habits held by people within a culture.
- Ethics refers to how the characteristics of ethos are enacted in terms of moral values and associated behavior. Ethics articulates and transports the concepts of ethos into practical actions.
- Aesthetics is the translation of ethics by means of artistic creativity. The aesthetics of a traditional culture is recognizably

culture-specific, although contemporary artists are moving toward a more global style of expression.

Two additional concepts, cultural relativism and situational ethics, will enhance our cultural literacy:

- Cultural relativism calls for disposing ethnocentric attitudes and giving equal legitimacy to other cultures' right to uniqueness.
- Situational ethics is a vital concept for the practice of cultural relativism. It refers to the right thing to do within the context of a specific circumstance. We practice situational ethics when we discover a situation that calls for behavior in conflict with our personal values. Embracing situational ethics means we are flexible and willing to shift views according to the demands of changing contexts.[1]

In the early 20th century, adventurous young Westerners traveled to Asia and the Middle East in search of their own identity. They returned with stories, fantastic and incredible, often catching an earful at home. Books from the 1920s and 30s contained romantic descriptions with exaggerated characterizations of exotic and different peoples and customs. While the literature excited the curiosity of readers who'd stayed home, it also reinforced Eastern and Western stereotypes in its portrayal of unfamiliar customs. Such stereotypes die hard.

Remnants of a Western attitude of Asians as the "other" are apparent in American media, which still refer to Asians as "non-Western." While no insult is intended, such linguistic quirks clearly reveal a built-in suspicion or fear of the other. This other, referred to as "them," in turn distances "us" from the unknown. How would Westerners feel about being designated "non-Eastern"?

The East-West paradigm has perpetuated this "other" attitude from antiquity. From ancient records, whether Chinese or Greek, we see foreigners referred to as "barbarians." Closer to home, when immigrants from the Old World colonized America, they perceived the native inhabitants as "red Indians"—savages—rather than indigenous First Nation people.

These opinions are held by those who consider themselves as belonging to one of the two: the self, as the insider, or the other, the outsider. Inevitably the foreigner is assigned negative attributes. In the minds of Eastern individuals, regardless of education or social standing, the image of the West oscillates from one extreme to the other. Opinions range from viewing Westerners as colonialists exploiting people and their resources, to new cultural imperialists who impose their way of life on others. On the opposite end of the spectrum, the same Westerners represent hopes and dreams of life in a paradise of self-determination, freedom, and affluence. The imagery chosen varies from period to period, depending on the political and economic situation of the perceiver.

Though colonialism belongs to the past, it's interesting to observe that the West, even today, has a far greater presence in the mind of Asians than vice versa. Another fascinating phenomenon is that when Westerners show interest in knowing more about Asia they turn to studying its traditional past, whereas Asian students of the West want to learn about its postmodern present.

Cultures, just like people, change over time—some faster than others. Western cultures during the last 50 years have altered drastically, with each passing year bringing exponential change. In order to cope with the changes in cultural realities, we ourselves have to change. An awareness of the underlying structure of culture is imperative to facilitating these changes. As we experience foreign cultures through friendships and travels, we soon realize that culture is not a thing but a process.

An army of scholars has published research explaining these processes. One theory authored by the much-maligned anthropologist Dr. Margaret Mead identifies three aspects of the role tradition plays in understanding a culture.[2] I've modified these categories as past-oriented, present-oriented, and future-oriented. This model is based on the following three considerations: 1) how the youth in each category locate authority figures; 2) where the culture finds it in the modernization process; 3) how these factors predicate young people's conceptions of reality as circumscribed by familial interrelationships and expected behavior.

1. A culture is past-oriented when its authority resides in the elders. Youth ask their grandparents' advice and permission before embarking on new endeavors. The past stands as an ideal model

and a major directive force in daily decision-making. Every effort is made to preserve traditions. Change is perceived as undesirable. Example: An adult needs the elders' permission to marry the person of his or her own choice.

2. A culture is present-oriented when its youth recognize their parents as the locus of authority, seeking their advice before embarking on new endeavors. Today, generation gaps are widening. Parents keep control over their children's activities as long as possible. Though not directly hostile to change, parents are slow to adjust to change, and consequently youth are less given to experimental and adventurous behavior. Change is acceptable when necessary. Example: "Be careful!"

3. A culture is future-oriented when its authority is invested in the self. Youth show overt disregard of the past, considering even their parents to be obsolete. Children of the computer age are teaching their parents and grandparents, reversing the pattern of bygone generations. Members of the younger generations have their own peer culture, seeking the advice of their peers and keeping their own counsel. As they don't feel the weight of history, they experiment and explore the unknown, undeterred by historic limitations and failures. They're poised to create a future driven by anger and fueled by the challenge of the impossible. Change is necessary and desirable. Example: "Don't trust anyone over 30."

The above distinctions are, of course, overgeneralized. We'll find that most cultures operate in varying degrees in each category. In the huge population of Third World countries, where the percentage of youth is very high, the gap between generations is extreme. There, categories 3 and 1 prevail. In Europe on the other hand, we'll more often than not find a combination of categories 2 and 3. In America category 3 is dominant, with considerable presence of category 2. However, category 1 is well represented in some rural areas and immigrant communities.

To recap, cultural literacy hinges on understanding a culture's ethos. As we've discussed, ethos provides the theoretical and philosophical underpinning that pertains to a culture's value system, derived from core concepts. Furthermore, a culture's ethos influences its members' conduct and actions. Similarly, to the same degree that people are able to translate a culture's ethos into ethics, or moral behavior, they also aspire to translate these values in aesthetic terms in their art. In other words, aesthetic expression in art is the visual counterpart to a culture's ethics, both stemming from the same value system. By appraising a culture's or an individual's aesthetics through art, we may likewise infer their ethos.

The following sections examine the interplay of culture as a collection of theoretical constructs and individual experience. Our aim in exploring these concepts is to graduate from personal, monocultural experience to conscious participation in the dynamics of multicultural coexistence.

Finding Cultural Common Denominators

A culture's ethos is an umbrella concept that is held aloft by the culture. That each spoke of the umbrella has been assented to by a majority of members of the culture is a given. Culture, unlike nature, is a wholly human-made construct; as such, its dynamics compound our challenge of understanding its complexities. Still, a culture can be viewed as a living organism, in that it's constantly changing and responding to the influences of neighboring cultures. These influences, ranging from wars, commerce, and technical innovations, are historically defined by space and time. Today the primary influence is seen through the interconnectedness afforded through the universal use of the World Wide Web.

In the past, when studying an unfamiliar culture we searched for the exotic. Today we seek the familiar in the unfamiliar and begin with identifying similarities. We are all cultural nomads, at times perceived even by some in our own multicultural society as foreigners. Yet, we try to overcome the distance that separates us. Only after we've acknowledged our common denominators through the identification of our respective core concepts do we have a baseline from which to focus on our differences.

Core concepts are defined by a culture's interactions with its belief systems. They encompass concepts of time and death, and of course concepts of relationships between family members—husband and wife, children, the elderly, and others. As we discover the distinction between core concepts and culture-specific concepts, we realize that, whereas core concepts are universal properties of any culture, the particular content of these core concepts isn't. Each culture designates the core concepts with aspects that are unique to its specific cultural identity. No culture can survive without distinct culture-specific characteristics. That said, we shouldn't be surprised to find more denominators that we share with other cultures than those that separate us.

Differences found in various cultures, which we refer to as culture-specificities, represent the values each culture invests in core concepts, making it possible for us for example to recognize Chinese culture as Chinese or American culture as American. Over time, cultures have been categorized into large divisions as seen from different perspectives, such as geographic (East/West), linguistic (Indo Arian/Semitic), religious (Judeo-Christian, Islamic), or political (democratic/dictatorial).

Typical of our time, economic criteria are widely used as means to define cultures. This insensitivity, though it may be inadvertent, is deeply imbedded in Western media coverage. We daily encounter reports where peoples of the world are designated Third World, originally defined as underdeveloped, and more recently as developing nations with low standards of living. This category clearly differentiates the "have nots" from the "haves." Today, these terms have gone from being mere descriptors of economic realities to foregone conclusions of cultural inferiority. Perhaps users of this terminology are not conscious of the underpinning assumption that linking economic concepts with cultural concepts assumes that higher economic standards indicate cultural superiority. The terms First World (superpower) and Second World (Europe) are rarely used. The Fourth World connotes natives within a country and include such groups as the indigenous First Nation people in the USA, the Ainu in Japan, or the Inuit of Canada, all of whom have preserved distinct cultures of their own.

A nostalgic residual from colonial times, our economically imposed division of the world reflects cultural bigotry born of perceived superiority—a cultural imperialism more insidious than blatant colonial imperialism because it assumes the inherent supremacy of Western thought in every regard.[3]

Identifying Cultural Specificities

What type of information helps us understand a specific culture? What does a person with a Euro-American frame of reference really need to understand in order to be able to access another culture? Is it the same knowledge that a person with a Pan-Asian frame of reference would consider essential? In all likelihood, no. What either of them would want to know is likely quite different. The questions raised are already culturally biased, insofar as we each use our own culture as a platform from which to view other cultures.

Just as each individual is unique, so is each culture. Finding what best describes an entire culture is problematic, as the answer is relative to the questioner. For some, Afghan culture conjures the weaving of rugs and tapestries. Some associate Islamic culture with calligraphy. Youth the world over identify American culture entirely by its popular culture. Broadly speaking, a culture is its people, in combination with what they do and how they interact. In the West, for example, the concept of individualism is defined as the ability to act independently, or as Alexis de Tocqueville found it, to "cultivate a way of life that depends on receiving nothing from anyone else and owing nothing to anyone else."[4] On the other hand, Confucian-inspired cultures (China, Japan, Korea, and parts of South East Asia including Vietnam and Malaysia) give priority to the collective, cultivating the art of interdependence between individuals, and between individuals and society at large. In these cultures, ideally speaking, group loyalty comes before individual interests. Despite the philosophical differences between individualism and collectivism, any culture can be viewed from the perspective of how it treats the weakest segments of the population—the old, the sick, the mentally challenged, and the children. Of course, the possible approaches to studying a culture are innumerable; we'll limit our discussion here to a few of the more salient points.

In our discussion of culture-specific characteristics, we'll focus on societal core concepts in relation to the following four areas: time, religion, family, and food. Each of these aspects contains essential data that provide insights into the character of that culture.

Time

How does a culture express its concept of time? The Christian calendar year 2008 is 4706 in the Chinese calendar, 1427 in the Islamic calendar, and 5769 in the Jewish calendar. Fundamental differences between cultures lie not only in their calendars, but in their views of history as well. Take, for example, those of India and China, two major societies of Asia: India has an organic, cyclical approach to history, which consists of an idealized narration of the heroic deeds of gods and man as expressed in epics, myths, and legends; the Chinese view history as linear, as an unfolding of events in time, recorded in chronological order and written down in thousands of annals. These annals were so reliable that even today Indian historians frequently consult Chinese documents to verify certain aspects of Buddhist history. Interestingly, the Greeks, and Western civilization at large, share this linear view of history.

Time, as negotiated in daily living, is indicative of the differences between theory and practice. Cultures measure time in experiential terms; therefore, how a culture relates to time also reveals dimensions of that culture's psyche and biorhythm. Since industrialization, clock time has replaced the older notion of time as cyclical, in tune with natural rhythms. Time has many properties: biological, psychological-personal, and sacred or metaphysical, to name a few. Presently, technology-based cultures are exploring the cyber-space concept of virtual time. Parallel universes and multiple realities are no longer perceived as pure science fiction, but are being explored by scientists and artists alike.

In modern technocratic cultures, the importance accorded to clock time has become one of the most defining elements of culture. In these cultures, time punctuates reality as if it were tangible, measurable, and fixed. Time has become something we can earn, spend, save, or waste. Urban 21st-century life has us believing that time is money. Just compare the fast-paced culture of metropolitan urban living in either New York or Beijing. There is a clear convergence of work and leisure in the technocratic hubs throughout the world, indicating that the concept of time also seems to be undergoing a globalization process.

Especially in the West, "wasting time," that is, using time counterproductively, has earned the lowly status of moral failure by authors from Benjamin Franklin to Stephen R. Covey.[5] In places where time and money are less dramatically linked, losing time is less of a concern. In some cultures, in fact, small tasks or the time in between them are willfully prolonged, and time spent on human interaction, or simply being, is highly valued; meal time in southern European cultures provides a widely recognized example. When among friends from different parts of the world, we notice differences between how individuals deal with time. Time, indeed, is one of the most significantly distinguishing dimensions of a culture.

Religion

Religion is another core concept that defines culture. If we look at religion as the spiritual history of human individuals, a study of religious practices in the monotheistic cultures of Judeo-Christian and Islamic traditions reveals an approach paralleling their linear concept of history. The study of polytheistic religions requires a more complex approach. It doesn't necessarily follow, however, that a society's linear approach to history presupposes a monotheistic view. A case in point is the Chinese, who, while subscribing to polytheism, also embrace a linear historical view and multiple religious systems.

Polytheism, a belief system of multiple gods, is inclusive. It also can mean that a person who lives in a polytheistic society may submit to several coexisting belief systems, revealing that various religious practices overlap, with no clear cut boundaries between them, such as practiced in India.

Unlike the exclusive approach practiced in monotheistic cultures, religious categories in polytheistic cultures defy quantification, since worshippers easily practice religious rituals and traditions culled from various belief systems from within their culture. Another example is the Japanese, many of whom celebrate birth with Shinto rituals, marriage with Christian rituals, and death with Buddhist rituals.

If challenged, people, cultures, and nations will claim that they live by a specific code of ethics. The biblical admonition, "Do to others, as you would have them do to you," is expressed in the five major world religions as variations of the same theme, the Chinese version being, "Do not do to others what you would not want others to do to you."[6]

Put those claims to the test and what do we find? Subscribing to a particular belief system doesn't necessarily correspond with actual behavior. Take for example the case of the USA, predominately a Christian nation. The biblical imperative, "Thou shalt not kill," theoretically established the sacredness of human life, yet Common Era Western civilization presents a litany of continuous engagement in warfare. Logically speaking, either Christianity doesn't meaningfully hold human life as sacred as Christianity prescribes, or Americans haven't entirely adopted Christian morals. This discrepancy between belief and reality is not unique to the USA. Because humans are human, the gap between theoretical and practical application persists. By examining an individual's or a culture's ethics and looking at how values are expressed through actions, we uncover to what extent the ethos is perceived as binding.

Family

Now let's examine the third core concept, family. We're currently witnessing changes in family structure all over the world. Traditionally, family referred to the extended family. The extended, multigenerational family provided economic and social support for its members, increasing their ability to survive and thrive. Each of the members contributed to the collective well-being of the family unit. The extended family is still the norm in many Third World countries. However, extended families are on the wane, since urban living emphasizes economic and individual independence. The nuclear family—an independent household of two parents and their children—became the next model.

A more recent variant is the single-parent family. Divorce is on the rise, and in some countries is obtainable without having to answer to its cause. In the USA, more than 60 percent of marriages end in divorce, in turn giving rise to the "blended family," which consists of two previously married individuals, each with children of their own, coming together to form a new family unit.[7] Children of blended families not only face difficulties in navigating their expanded relationships with stepparents and stepsiblings, they also face challenges related to being physically shuttled between households.

A loosening of traditional mores permits cohabitation of males and females without stigmatization of either partner. This trend, which began in the midst of the anonymity afforded in urban centers, is spreading globally. When children are born outside of wedlock, the mother often must assume the roles of father, mother, and sole provider, unless she gives the child up for adoption. The psychological consequences for these children, particularly boys growing up without a father, are not yet clearly understood.

Additional unconventional views on marriage are evident in the increasing social acceptance of same-sex partners. Contrary to traditional gender roles, same-sex partners are slowly gaining acceptance by the church and the state, including the right to marry and adopt children. But the leading social institution in this regard is the corporate world, which has become increasingly sensitive to discrimination issues. For example, to smooth over contentious public relations with the lesbian, gay, bisexual, and transgender (LGBT) community, the Walt Disney Company announced in 2007 that it would allow same-sex couples to hold "Fairy Tale Weddings" at its theme parks and on its cruises. Disney spokesperson Donn Walker emphasized the moral aspect, claiming that the decision was "consistent with our policy of creating a welcoming, respectful, and inclusive environment for all of our guests."[8]

Food

Though there is no single specific medium that best expresses the voice of a culture—some propose music, others, art—I suggest food as perhaps the most widely celebrated cultural identifier. Together with the fascinating ingredients and customs surrounding it, from fasting to festivals, food serves as a rewarding vehicle for examining culture-specific characteristics.

Food reveals the collage of influences that a culture has passed through over time, as well as where the culture belongs in the spectrum of tradition and modernity. Food is a universal commodity, and sharing food is a celebrated form of socialization in every culture. In China you're greeted not with "Hello, how are you?" but with "*Che fan-le mei you?*" ("Have you eaten yet?").

Some of us will never forget the regular meals at home or the commotion around preparation of special delicacies and the smell of baking on holidays, when the entire family sat for hours eating together. Throughout one's life, mother's cooking and the associated dietary conventions are calming reminders of one's familial and cultural roots.

Every experienced cook realizes that in the eating ritual, it's not only the food that counts; how food is prepared and how it is served, together with the aesthetics of the surroundings, are just as important. Ambiance embraces all aspects of the visual contexts together, creating an atmosphere that defines a culture's traditional identity. Food selections and preparations are distinguishing features of ethnic differences.

In countries where deprivation of food belongs to intermittent life experiences, we find elaborate decorum surrounding dinner table customs. Take for example the Ethiopian custom of giving *gursha.* The meal begins with a large communal platter lined with wedges of sponge bread. Instead of using metal utensils or wooden chopsticks, Ethiopians use the sponge bread to sop up a mouthful, and in a ritual gesture, feed the person sitting next to them.

As Lévi-Strauss and others have convincingly argued, we can find parallel homologies in institutions of any given culture, at any given time, that reflect and illuminate one another. In other words, we can expect to find an analogy between the culture of food within a country and that of its other cultural expressions. There is a principle at work here that I call the *constancy of similar differences*. Considering this principle may be helpful when we become overwhelmed trying to compare cultures in regard to their differences. The constancy of similar differences proposes that when you discover an area of expression that is culture-specific, it's reasonable to expect the presence of a similar level of specificity in other areas of expression within that culture—differences pertaining to time, religion, family, food, people, fashion, and the arts. The constancy of similar differences applies to the study of one culture in particular as well as cross-culturally.

Here's a cross-cultural example of the constancy of similar differences: The Chinese traditionally eat with chopsticks, which allows them to determine the size and single out the kinds of food that go into each mouthful.[9] We see a similar degree of deliberation and moderation in the traditional Chinese art aesthetic. Colors, for example, like emotions, are understated, although the range and variations of black through white typically exhibit great sophistication. Depictions of people follow a conventional decorum: usually a male in a formal position, in attire that covers the entire body. Now, compare this aesthetic with a culture whose members traditionally used their fingers to eat with rather than chopsticks.

Indian art expresses colorful arrays of emotion, both in miniature paintings and in sculpture. Women frequently appear as subjects, depicted with an uninhibited sense of appreciation of their feminine forms. Is it not plausible that this culture's aptitude for sensuous experiences, such as fingers daily touching the different textures of food brought to the mouth, would also find expression in its art?

The constancy of similar differences, as defined above, is perhaps easier to grasp if you look into fast food restaurants as a reflection of contemporary American culture. You can go to any franchise—McDonald's, Kentucky Fried Chicken, Baskin-Robins—and find that these fast, convenient, streamlined, standardized, comparatively affordable eateries, with their aesthetics of mass-produced plastic utensils and paper napkins, exhibit aspects typical of the contemporary urban, hurried, throw-away American culture? Here, the concept central to American culture, "time is money," is illustrated by the availability of fast food, also central to American lifestyle.[10]

The global proliferation of American fast food franchises provides yet another example of a convergence of cultures' core concepts. While this transformation offers an expansion of choices, we find a homogenization in terms of the choices themselves: It is truly wonderful to find a French baguette in Tokyo, but eat at an upscale restaurant, and we could as likely be in New York as in Johannesburg. Does Thai food in Los Angeles or in New Delhi really taste identical to the food served in Bangkok? Adjusted to meet the taste of an international palette, Thai food found outside of Thailand will more than likely sacrifice a measure of authenticity.

That said, we can still learn much about a culture by visiting the local ethnic restaurants and partaking in a traditionally prepared meal. I believe our next assigned experiment will be easy for most readers to swallow—see "Tasting Cultures" in appendix A on page 132.

By learning to approach other cultures with patience, sensitivity, and respect for cultural specificities, we can avoid misunderstandings and cross-cultural blunders. Even if we harbor a preference for the specificities of our primary culture, we have little to lose and much to gain from interacting with foreigners—whether on our home turf or theirs.

Mapping Cultural Response Phases

We learn about and respond to a culture in an incremental process in which each step has its own format and characteristics. Some of us have walked every step as part of our life experiences; others haven't yet had the opportunity. In this section we'll discuss some of these steps, with an emphasis on those that normally are part of only the immigrant experience. As multicultural individuals, it's pertinent that we make ourselves aware of the hardships endured by certain individuals while climbing these steps. Each of us maintains a kind of multicultural consciousness, meaning that we not only belong to a parent culture comprised of nationality, tradition, and ethnicity, but we also have a personal culture, that is, a culture we define for ourselves through our perceptual processes—a culture unique to each of us as individuals. Without awareness of either culture, we needlessly limit our modes of perception. This limitation preconditions the way we see, analyze, and respond to data. Our ingrained and habitual modes of perception and interaction may work well within familiar arenas, but once outside, will we know how to survive, let alone thrive? What model can we look to in our newly discovered need of cultural literacy?

Open our eyes, and we'll see our models all around us.

As discussed above, enculturation is a process that everyone experiences from his or her earliest stage of being. Acculturation follows, the maturation process, moving from childhood into adulthood. This is further experienced when changing domicile from one culture to another. Once an immigrant arrives in a new nation, experiences vary contingent on the country of origin, age, gender, religion, education, language, profession, and economic circumstance. Acculturation is most poignantly experienced by immigrants; it becomes increasingly difficult the more their primary language and religion diverge from those of the host culture. For most immigrants the final step is assimilation, indicating that the adopted culture has taken precedence over their birth culture.

Enculturation

Enculturation begins at birth. It's the first step we take in a life-long journey. It represents an intense socialization process, in which a child imbibes its culture through the various ducts of its environment. These ducts instill the child with the substance of its culture's ethos. For those who continue to live solely within their birth culture, what's learned through the enculturation process is usually enough to resolve questions like "Who am I, and how am I supposed to fit in with my own people?"

In the earliest phase, children who learn to speak don't choose their language; rather, they acquire their native tongue through the avenue of subconscious absorption. In the same manner, the child absorbs like mother's milk what is considered right and wrong. During the enculturation process, the child learns what it takes to become a good person, a bad person, and any number of persons in between.

Enculturation constitutes the platform from which a person, society, or culture formulates its way of thinking and acting. The ethos, as previously discussed, is the metaconcept for the mores, rules, values, and tastes that become as it were a person's skin. It's through the enculturation process that one learns to adopt the core concepts discussed above. A culture's ethos represents its vision of reality and is articulated either verbally or non-verbally by conscious actions or unconscious reactions in response to specific situations. The effect of core concepts from the perspective of their influence upon an individual is comparable to the water in which fish swim. Just as fish take for granted the natural liquid environment, so also individuals, within their own cultural environment, are unconscious of the implications, assuming that what's natural for them is natural for everyone.

Because of their very nature, cultural assumptions belong to the domain of the things we take for granted. We'll consider these assumptions as the uncontested foundation of conventional, self-evident attitudes that we enact in *a priori* judgments. In other words, these assumptions function as presumptions, yet when they surface, and we act on them, they're perceived particularly by outsiders as prejudice.

The family is the primary source of a child's encounter with the content of a culture's core concepts, instilled through a natural passive digestion. However, what one culture believes to be correct may be taboo or unacceptable in another. It appears that all of us, whether we're conscious of it or not, have elements of prejudice to a greater or lesser degree. People may mean no harm, but through no fault of their own they've been enculturated with specific beliefs. In the words of a student, "I've become less prejudiced toward other cultures and their ways of thinking or perceiving, as I strive to control my judgments by trying to see from another's point of view. It is also beneficial to realize that persons from other cultures in all likelihood judge me and place me under stereotypes in the same manner."

Customarily, we're unaware of how deeply we're anchored in our cultural heritage, and that our perceptions are informed by our enculturation experiences. In a tradition-oriented society, the "cultural DNA" are especially controlling in cementing an individual's personality down to the smallest detail. What we take for granted keeps us trapped in familiar thought patterns or assumptions, unless we recognize them for what they are, namely, unconsciously held mental habits. These assumptions preempt our abilities to meet the unfamiliar with an open, nonjudgmental attitude.[11]

Acculturation

Acculturation is a process usually associated with immigrants. In reality, acculturation simply refers to the modification of lifestyles and specific cultural traits induced by changing environments. This could take place through migration within a country, through cross-cultural and/or interracial marriages, or simply as a maturation process. One type of acculturation manifests itself in the individuating steps adolescents take in an effort to distance themselves from parental supervision.

During the enculturation process, parents and additional authority figures—teachers, police, and others—are often perceived as agents of unjust power, constricting freedom. Teens, typically characterized by mood-swings and personal turbulence, must negotiate the period between adolescence and adulthood, which generally spawns a desire to migrate from the safety of the childhood home to the challenges of the world at large.

What immigrants experience in terms of acculturation is comparable to what adolescents encounter, but adapting to a foreign culture, learning a new language and new ways of conduct, can be even more dramatic. Though the two processes are similar, one significant difference is, what a native teen had years to sort out, an immigrant must begin immediately on arrival. The acculturation experience frequently begins with culture shock,[12] in large part because so many cultural mores, and manners of expressing them verbally, must be relearned.

Immigrants, in spite of all of the various circumstances causing them to leave their countries, fall into two categories: those who acculturate and those who assimilate. All immigrants learn to accommodate to the host culture without necessarily giving up the emotional priority to the culture in which they were enculturated. In this way, immigrants who stay in touch with their own cultural roots through their extended family, mother tongue, religious festivals, and food, eventually become bicultural as they adapt to the new culture.

When possible, many first-generation immigrants ease the transition into their new surroundings by moving into areas where immigrants of their own ethnicity have already settled. The greater the differences between their own culture and the host culture, the greater immigrants feel the need to affirm their position as outsiders by seeking ties with an existent local self-segregated community.[13]

A person's move from one environment or culture to another is sometimes associated with loneliness and various other difficulties of acclimatization. For every individual, the acculturation process, no matter how intense, is a process that involves familiarity with two distinct experiences: the initial culture shock, and its subsequent transformative phase of compromising and adjusting.

Culture shock is a transitory state of mind experienced not only by immigrants, but also by students studying abroad. Anyone who has to face the numerous unexpected situations when trying to negotiate and function in culturally unfamiliar terrain will most likely experience culture shock to a greater or lesser degree. The less prepared are most defenseless since they lack coping skills to deal with behavioral challenges outside their own comfort zone.

Culture shock leaves one feeling that circumstances have passed beyond his or her control. It builds insecurity and diminishes self-esteem, because the accustomed responses and familiar symbols of social intercourse have disappeared. In that situation, one must learn basic behavioral patterns anew.

Intense discomfort sets in when known personal frames of reference, anchored as they are in one's cultural heritage, no longer apply to situations in an unfamiliar culture. Everything is strange—from the language, to the food, to strangers' unpredictable behavior. The disorientation that follows is a natural response to the loss of the stabilizing mirror that reflects one's self-image, the image held by one's peers, and by those known and seen daily. Hence the French adage, *"partir c'est mourir un peu"* (leaving is dying a bit).

An effective remedy against the first impact of culture shock is to let go of the habit of looking for what is different in the host culture from one's own. Only if one is willing to accept without criticizing can one begin to assess and calibrate the common denominators between the cultures. From that platform, one can move to consciously register what distinguishes each, and learn to face differences with self-control intact.

One cure for culture shock is to get involved in the foreign culture and search for its signifiers. We begin by identifying the culture-specific content of its core concepts. In the process, we see our own culture from a new perspective, particularly when people of the host country ask us about our country of origin. Responding to such inquiries deepens our understanding of our own culture, allowing us to more clearly comprehend the similarities and differences of the other. The questions we generate and respond to allow us to see ourselves from the inside-out and vice versa, which eventually frees us from the "us vs. them" dualism. Of course, this give-and-take presupposes an ability to communicate through an interpreter, if not through a common language.

Traveling abroad provides a great venue for coming to understand certain aspects of our own culture. It's helpful to start by listening to the questions raised by people foreign to our culture. Through the responses we get to the answers we give, we begin to perceive our own culture through the eyes of others. Slowly, we become conscious of those aspects of a culture that we normally take for granted, learning to recognizing the types of questions that crack the seeds of cultural assumptions.

Culture shock can happen not only when a traveler is abroad facing the unknown, but also on returning home. Because he or she has gained a better understanding of the mechanics of acculturation, the prodigal is prone to take offense at family members and peers who demonstrate a persistent lack of cultural awareness. This so-called reverse culture shock is sometimes felt even more strongly than the initial culture shock. Upon their return, travelers realize that it's they themselves who've changed, rather than those who stayed home; yet another attitudinal revision is sometimes in order to overcome the hurt and anger.

Some students returning home from years of studying abroad might find themselves total misfits, and the emotional trauma may be the more cruel because they don't know how to bridge the gap between their youthful idealism and the reality of available opportunities. This gap can be particularly ominous for Third World students returning from the hardship of adjusting to modernized societies, for which they've already paid a high acculturation price.

Culture shock, reverse or otherwise, can be mitigated through greater awareness of the enculturation and acculturation processes. Once the traveler has processed and understood the content of enculturation, it's easier to acknowledge that the content of core concepts is culture-specific—learned, rather than innate. The seasoned traveler understands what he or she needs to know about an unfamiliar culture before encountering it.

Situational Ethics

Once the initial culture shock has lost its numbing grip, the individual can adapt and adjust by modifying his or her behavior. By necessity, life in a multicultural society is fraught with situations that have the potential for leading to conflict. For those deeply committed to their own cultural values, the concept of situational ethics can be particularly problematic. Situations need to be approached in context and from several perspectives. A practiced sense of cultural relativity is vital when a new situation demands flexibility, especially when a necessary course of action comes into conflict with cultural values imbedded from birth. Situational ethics implies a willingness to shift views according to the demands of any given situation.

What is correct in one context or culture may not be so in another. Changes in time and place often require that we put our personal opinions aside to accommodate the new situation, as expressed in the aphorism, "When in Rome, do as the Romans do." This statement, of course, is easier said than done, and acclimating to unfamiliar cultures can give rise to a number of psychological problems. The severity of the ensuing problems varies and depends on the disparity between the host and guest cultures; the motivation, moral agenda, and sincerity of the immigrant; and the degree that the immigrant feels welcome in the host country. Many immigrants feel like outsiders throughout their lives, while their children grow up to become bicultural, developing an allegiance to their parents' birth culture and the culture they're raised in.

A nimble mind and an appetite for learning help narrow the gap between entrenched, counterproductive responses to unfamiliar circumstances, and productive adaptation to them. The "Exchanging Perspectives" exercise in appendix A on page 134 will challenge your ability to tolerate and adapt to diverse viewpoints.

Assimilation

Assimilation is the process of adopting another culture. Whereas acculturation is an exercise in survival techniques, assimilation is a matter of choice. Each of these avenues is a taxing process replete with trials and errors. All immigrants undergo an acculturation process, but not all assimilate. A decisive factor in assimilation is the original reason for immigrating. Was it political or economic, temporary or permanent? How does the host population respond to the immigrant? The greater the perceived foreignness of the immigrant, the more suspicion and prejudice he or she will meet. When immigrants are exposed to overt or covert hostilities, they may react in kind, making assimilation less likely.

Conceptualizing Coexisting Cultures

A multicultural society is defined not by separate countries, but by many cultures existing within a country. We frequently encounter people whose conduct and expectations are culture-specific, reflecting their ethnicity. As identifying designations, ethnicity and nationality are distinct. Nationality refers to the country that issues our passport; it's a temporal condition that can be changed. Ethnicity, on the other hand, identifies us within a social group whose members are distinguished by virtue of their common history, beliefs, values, habits, customs, and behavioral norms.

Encounters with monocultural individuals in multicultural social situations require that both parties practice awareness and flexibility in their responses and attitudes. The much-disputed concept of "political correctness" (PC) was endorsed by social institutions in the late 20th century to educate the public about the volatile effects certain words and expressions can carry. The idea was to sensitize people to their language usage and encourage a self-censuring consciousness, avoiding the articulation of either intended or unintended racial slurs or other expressions of pejorative attitudes. Rather than contending that if no hurt is intended, no hurt can be felt, PC is based on the linguistic theory that words in and of themselves influence thoughts and cultivate existing attitudes, in the same way that sexist language promotes sexist acts. PC became prevalent in university courses and political speeches, not only in the USA but also in numerous other Western countries. This movement toward broad social, political, and educational change had the intent of redressing historic injustices in matters such as race, class, gender, and sexual orientation. It's debatable, however that PC has had any consequential effect at the grass roots level, which could in reality be symptomatic of an entrenched unwillingness to address the deeper issues of racism and other types of discrimination.

Race is distinct from ethnicity, in that it's defined by physical DNA, while ethnicity describes a specific cultural affiliation, although today ethnicity is often viewed as a minority culture within a culture. The distinction between race and ethnicity is commonly blurred, and ethnic identity often invites blatant racism on the part of majority cultures and within the minority cultures themselves.[14]

The primary goal of a multicultural society is to avoid the type of political and cultural clashes amply demonstrated throughout history that can culminate in ethnic cleansing of minority groups. Hawaii and Singapore are frequently cited as examples of relatively successful multicultural societies. In these places we find a configuration of multiple ethnic groups of differing national origins, every citizen with their culture-specific core concepts intact, living in peaceful coexistence. All citizens no matter their origin are free to practice their cultural traditions as long as their behavior is lawful and doesn't impinge on others.

In multicultural societies immigrants are expected to behave in accordance to the mores of the host country. But even under the best of conditions a number of difficult problems can go unresolved. Such problems arise in several aspects of the immigrant experience, such as compliance with local administrative policies and interactions with members of the host culture.

By assimilating, immigrants reshape their entire lives to conform to the expectations of their adopted culture. For immigrants and their children, it's hard to overstate the complexities of becoming bicultural. Reconciling the countless dichotomies of a double heritage can sometimes necessitate the rejection of one culture's directives in favor of the other, which in turn can cause a great sense of loss. The term for such loss is *deculturation.* The crucial question is, does either party carry any more or less responsibility for accommodation than the other? Many members of the host culture tend to act on the belief that when the outsiders assimilate and become citizens through the "naturalization" process, only then do they become "normal" and worthy of being treated as equals. Americans might find it easier to accept immigrants if they were cognizant of the pain and effort immigrants endure. Multicultural societies require not only passive tolerance, but also active support.

The present political landscape the world over illustrates the inability of people with differing ethnic backgrounds to sustain harmonious relations. Scholars fill libraries with books proposing theories for peaceful multicultural coexistence. Whether the studies address the multinational world per se, or subsets of it, the conflicts they identify exhibit similar patterns. Though many authors point to religious and language differences as the primary cause of conflict, the majority see economics as the culprit, especially in times of financial instability.

Three prevalent conceptions of ideal multicultural societies include the melting pot, salad bowl, and tapestry models. As these models shape the expectations of host and immigrant cultures alike, it would be beneficial to briefly discuss the qualities and merits of each.

Melting Pot

From a historical point of view, America's cultural identity began with the ideal of a monoculture forged of European transplants. Immigrants from Western countries were welcomed with the understanding that they would assimilate and integrate into the culture of the new American society. The melting pot theory describes this expectation of merging cultures. It conjures up the image of a meal, prepared in a large cooking pot, delivering consistency, nourishment, and full flavor with every spoon full. Each ingredient contributes to the wholesome meal, just as each citizen contributes to the whole social fabric. In America's colonial history, immigration policy monitored by the local Caucasian population was defined not by cultural pluralism, but by the concept of an all-embracing monoculture. The ideal envisioned was to melt into one family, one language, one nation.

The dream of equality meshes with the nation's notion of the inalienable right to life, liberty, and the pursuit of happiness guaranteed each citizen. The dream of America as the land of opportunity promises education, great economic reward for hard work, and social mobility. In spite of periodic social unrest associated with its immigration policy, the USA continues to welcome immigrants from all over the world, albeit it with limitations on the number admitted annually.[15]

After two centuries, the melting pot model has become obsolete. Obviously, when immigrant populations hailed from cultures fairly similar to each other, acculturation and assimilation came easier. However, to expect all immigrants to behave and acclimatize to a new culture to the same extent, in the same way, or at the same rate is not realistic. In sum, the melting pot ideal has its own agenda; it's not a celebration of cultural diversity, but a repudiation of it.

Now that we understand the difficulties experienced by immigrants who insulate themselves in their own cultural enclaves, we need to ask what it would take for them to move out of their familiar social network and community of people who speak the same language and help each other. Understanding this often-traumatic transition alleviates alienation for the immigrant and the citizen alike. While living in an immigrant community is unquestionably advantageous during the early period of transition to the new culture, staying there can impair the acculturation process and lead to isolation.

Language gaps often result in mutual misunderstanding between host and immigrant populations. Ignorance of available resources can cause immigrants' needs to go unmet, and language problems can also limit participation in governance and voting. To encourage immigrant communities to vote on issues concerning them, California has made ballots available in Chinese, Japanese, Khmer (Kamay), Spanish, and Vietnamese. Shifting the paradigm from melting pot to one of cultural pluralism indicates a society's acceptance of diversity as the desirable status quo—multiculturalism in praxis.

Salad Bowl

The salad bowl multicultural model has to a large extent superseded the earlier melting pot model. The idea of the salad bowl is not to give up one's original culture by melting into mainstream. Rather, the salad bowl honors differences so that, as in a salad bowl, we can pick from a variety of lettuces, fruits, vegetables, or seeds, each retaining its original character and flavor. The salad bowl concept still requires some effort for an immigrant to adjust to; the recipe calls for a period of social acclimatization, but acculturation suffices—assimilation is not required.

Similar to the notion of political correctness, the salad bowl idea has received much criticism from cultural conservatives who demand nothing less than complete assimilation. At its very best, multiculturalism seeks to eradicate racism. However, the Los Angeles-based Ayn Rand Institute opposes multiculturalism, which it sees as a threat to "the superiority of Western Civilization." An institute newsletter warns, "Far from being a cure for racism, multiculturalism is racism in a new, self-righteous guise."[16]

Tapestry

Where melting pot advocates expect immigrants to assimilate and thereby discard their particular traditions and language, the tapestry model asserts the right of diverse cultures to proliferate and flourish in a self-determined fashion. This model presupposes an emotional maturity that allows us to respect the values of other cultures in addition to our own. Just as the political correctness movement attempted to accomplish in creating awareness of our speech patterns, the tapestry model encourages us to break the mold of assimilation by recognizing and disowning cultural bias, bigotry, or any form of "centrism." Through education, we come to understand that asserting cultural superiority over another equally relevant group actually discourages acculturation and is no longer a viable modus operandi.[17]

In the past, history and literature were the primary sources for learning cultural diversity, but today our visual environment and the community become the laboratory for culture research. In reality, there's much work to be done in the area of attitude shifts.

For many immigrants from South East Asia and the Middle East, becoming Americanized means losing their original identity. A case in point are Buddhists, who face violating their ethics simply by doing what it takes to make it in America. Consider the inner turmoil a Buddhist faces in entering into the fierce competition characteristic of American professional life. The aggressive self-promotion practiced on the road to success repulses many Buddhists, whose ethics place cooperation in the interest of the collective above the struggle for individual hegemony that defines the American mythos.[18]

Muslims meet similar conflicts in trying to maintain the integrity of their values when adjusting to life in the mainstream culture, particularly in respect to women and their position. The freedom with which women move about and participate on all levels of life in Western societies is considered immoral within some sectarian Islamic traditions. For example, in order to preserve their values, Muslim fathers will forbid their daughters to date, and demand that they wear the hijab, or traditional veil, as a declaration of submission to the faith.

Cultures express socially acceptable behaviors pervasively through their media, monitored by their respective codes, whether creatively through the arts, or in more calculated approximations interpreted by marketing gurus. With so many coexisting cultures, a homogeneous stew is an unrealistic ideal. It's far too simplistic and reactionary for any ever-shrinking majority to demand that "if you don't like our way of life, you can get the hell out." Our challenge is not to cleanse culture of its diversity, but rather to find a balance that honors the diversity that each culture brings to the table.

The above models that shape national attitudes toward immigration paint a picture of the "culture wars" that have accompanied the economic globalization trends of the late 20th and early 21st centuries. It's true that cultural conservatives and liberals like to blame each other for the social upheaval immigration invariably stirs. However, since the first time a hominid quit his or her camp to take up with another, the genie has been out of the bottle, and intractable attitudes won't coax it back in. Cultural literacy proposes solutions to the dilemma of balancing diverging belief systems and fostering tolerance. As hard as the lesson may come for some, we must all grasp the meaning of cultural relativity before we can learn to acknowledge and appreciate cultural diversity.

Are we truly living up to the challenge of living in a multicultural society? Mainstream interest in learning intercultural communication seems to come to a standstill at the interpersonal level. As an Hispanic artist acquaintance remarked, "When it comes to learning about different cultures, Caucasians are willing to experiment with ethnic foods and observe ethnic festivals, buy ethnic clothing and even art. But when it comes to including immigrants as friends, most hesitate, while culturally literate individuals yearn for the reverse."

In response to a discussion in my "Cross Cultural Visual Literacy" course, one student expressed his reluctance to embrace multiculturalism with an allusion to the sorrow of deculturation, the loss of one's indigenous cultural identity: "It feels that if I were to understand all cultures and be ethical and sensitive, I would lose my own identity. I would eventually become but a mirror to please all who come my way."

Another student, in response to the question, "What is my position in my culture?" wrote, "I am a WASP, white Anglo-Saxon Protestant. You could also add that I am a male, so I guess that puts me into the 'bad-guy' group that has created an intolerant society that has held back women and minorities since the Dark Ages."

So we see that the fear of losing one's identity, cultural bearings, even the pieces of one's historical narrative that aren't much to brag about, is a very real concern for members of the mainstream culture as well as the newcomers.

Even after immigrants and their progeny have become American citizens and, by choice, have assimilated, have they automatically become part of the mainstream, or do they still feel excluded to a degree? As a test, pose this question to an African-American, a Mexican-American, a Chinese-American, or any other "hyphenated" American. Exponents of mainstream cultural opinions would deny that color discrimination is still an issue. However, we only need to look at statistics regarding educational opportunities and other inequities in economic status to know that an average black household annually earns about $20,000 less than that of an average white household.

Gross discrimination is seen even more clearly in the substandard working conditions and wages of undocumented workers. This situation, a de facto legalization of both their social status and their economic exploitation, is reprehensible in any country claiming democracy and human rights as its moral virtues, let alone the richest nation in the world.

Considering the personal sacrifice and social upheavals associated with immigration, it would seem at first glance that no reward could be worth the misery. Economic realities being what they are, however, perhaps we can best understand immigrants' motivation by paraphrasing Swiss author and Nobel Prize winner Hermann Hesse, with a slight embellishment: Better to be a foreigner among foreigners, than a [poor] stranger among one's own.

Assessing Dynamics of Multiculturalism

What impact do immigrants have on their host cultures, and how do host cultures impact the immigrants? Worldwide, guest worker programs provide obvious economic benefits. Yet problems associated with these programs go unresolved. Often guest workers migrate from developing nations, and after their contracts are up some prefer to stay in the host country, hoping for acceptance as economic refugees. Additional immigrants with or without valid documentation simply arrive with no intention of leaving.

The current situation in the USA isn't unlike what several European countries have experienced during the last several decades. Numbering in the millions, so-called illegal immigrants live in constant fear of arrest and/or deportation. While countries cope with the reality of the situation in different ways, the commonality of the problem lies in the fact that huge numbers of newcomers further strain infrastructures whose resources are already stretched.

In the USA an estimated 12 million undocumented immigrants, most from Mexico and Central and South America, fill a niche in the agricultural, construction, and service industries. Advocates argue that, legal or not, these workers are indispensible to the economy. On the other hand, by their sheer number these immigrants place additional stress on health and educational institutions, causing a growing number of Americans to take umbrage at the idea of subsidizing these services for people who have no legal claim to them. Emergency rooms are inundated by uninsured patients who have nowhere else to turn; overcrowded classrooms take in children of immigrants, 46 percent of whom speak languages other than English at home, and teachers have to cope with any of the more than 100 languages spoken.

Tempers have also flared in Europe between host countries and guest workers, the majority of whom are Muslim. Islam, with 1.2 billion adherents dispersed around the globe, presents further challenges due to its divergent nature. Practicing Muslims experience conflicts in retaining the integrity of their own values while adjusting to the mainstream culture, especially in their sense that contemporary Western culture is corrupting.

One way immigrants seek to defend and reassert their cultural identity is to build religious structures that more often than not are very foreign to the local landscape. One of the largest mosques outside the Middle East, planned for the outskirts of London, is experiencing great opposition from the locals, just as the large Buddhist Shi Lai and Hindu Venkateswara temples recently constructed in Southern California had met with strong opposition from local communities. The democratic process in both countries has overriding concerns, forcing an uneasy acceptance of such structures in suburban communities.

Even when attitude change begins with court-ordered tolerance, ideally we'll follow it up with compassion and acceptance of existing differences. In a broader perspective, the conflicts in pockets of American and European mainstream culture are minor compared to the clash of civilizations waged on the civilian battle fields of Gaza, Lebanon, Iraq, and Afghanistan.

Interestingly, the problems facing nations often mirror those of individuals, both in the types and patterns of conflicts. Whether addressing the reoccurring difficulties of multicultural coexistence on the national or local level, we all play a role in finding practical, peaceful solutions in our encounter with diversity. Never before has the world with its many problems been brought so close to our attention. While electronic mass media crisscrosses geophysical and cultural boundaries every day, people continue to struggle with dormant and defensive attitudes relating to cultural differences. Eventually we, either by default or concerted effort, will have to modify old habits of perception. The burden of learning to live with immigrants and other minority groups falls to each of us—even those for whom this acceptance doesn't come easily.

The question remains, how do we function effectively within a society with ever-present contradictory convictions threatening our quality of life without, in turn, threatening the quality of life of those who don't conform to the prevailing values and customs? No one in a pluralistic society can altogether avoid situations that invite such difficulties. Tolerance, widely accepted as the solution to the problem of the pluralistic challenge, is mandatory, but in and of itself it's still insufficient for those who hope for more than an uneasy coexistence. A deeper understanding is required, even to the extent of accepting that certain problems may not yield a cogent, one-size-fits-all solution. The divergent ideologies found in pluralistic societies require that we allow contradictory concepts to coexist without any one impinging over the other, recognizing each as a valid component of our multicultural reality.

By mere appearance, specific ethnic groups are recognized as such and marginalized by mainstream policies. The media perpetuate this situation by referring to cultures of ethnic groups as "subcultures," connoting a built-in inferiority compared to mainstream culture. In sum, pluralism embraces the concept of "live and let live." In the words of Professor Benjamin R. Barber, "The literacy required to live in civil society, the competence to participate in democratic communities, the ability to think critically and act deliberately in a pluralistic world, the empathy that permits us to hear and thus accommodate others, all involve skills that must be acquired."[19]

Living in a multicultural society requires each of us to commit to the inclusion of all. Most of us are a composite of several cultures as it is. In so many ways, we're all nomads and foreigners, even in our own multicultural society. We need not be immigrants, either of the first, second, or third generation, in order to be multicultural. Migration from one state or one part of the country to another, interethnic marriage, and traveling or living abroad all provide multicultural experiences. We have to stop demonizing other people, who, after all, are simply transcendental projections of ourselves.

There is a pattern here. Problems loom large when we address the dynamics of coexisting cultures, yet they're the same problems faced by ethnic groups coexisting within a single culture. We'll see the pattern repeated as we move from the concept of a multicultural America to an envisioned global culture.

5

Understanding Our Present and Creating Our Future

Compressing space by driving instead of walking; compressing time by channel surfing the air waves; satisfying our hunger instantly with ready-made food; these habits change our perception of reality by cutting away all of the inconveniences we used to endure before reaching our goals. One-night stands and making love on the first date reinforce the pattern. Consequently our ability to cope when things don't happen quickly enough, or to deal with the smaller details that have to be attended to, is diminishing. Intensely felt impatience leads to bad temper that can escalate into violence, as we see in the "road rage" phenomenon. The convergence of time and space driven by advancing technology, where space is restructured into shorter and shorter units, is incompatible with our natural physical and psychological rhythms. Theorists agree that this contraction of space, by time, has a personality-altering impact on people across the globe, even if the effects aren't yet fully understood.

We see a similar pattern in contemporary broadcast news reporting that frenetically shifts focus from country to country and event to event, spiced with bursts of sensationalism, in a constant narrative that distorts our perception of reality in 24/7 cycles.

The underpinning theme of this final chapter is education. As we've demonstrated in our study of art, people, and culture, education increases our ability to process and internalize new experiences and information. The unknown only becomes accessible when we place it in the context of what we already know; therefore, the broader our education, the greater our capacity to absorb new ideas. As the technical aspects of communications systems become more refined, information becomes even more accessible, leveling the playing field for everyone. Knowledge is power; the challenge now is to match emerging technology with an ethic that inspires a humane context in which to structure the content.

Viewing art involves reexperiencing events based on images that have been filtered through the mind of another person—the artist. The more aware we become of this process of give and take, the better prepared we are to distinguish between the power of suggestion and indoctrination.

Similarly, the role of education in the 21st century must be to prepare us to process information delivered through increasingly pervasive, all-encompassing mass media. Education must focus on interpretative skills and critical thinking, dealing with issues of mutual human concern as seen from a global perspective.

The challenge today is to integrate rapid-fire emotions with cognitive thinking in order to integrate information with knowledge. Just as in decoding art, we gain insight by interpreting information in context, so we need to be aware of the difference between knowledge and fact accumulation; since computer technology can both help and hinder our awareness and comprehension of this difference, it's central to this discussion.

The development of computers and the Internet is as revolutionary as Gutenberg's invention of the printing press. Here the comparison stops, however, because as the computer evolves into a more flexible and powerful tool, dipping into the capability of consciousness, intelligence, and emotional competencies, it assumes properties comparable to that of human cognition. We can't foresee every consequence such developments will have, but certain aspects of the role computers play are clear. Computers are indispensable in research and other labor-intensive tasks, providing specialists with a vast network of information to intersect emerging technologies in interdisciplinary research. Computers and other digital devices also connect casual users to the Internet, a limitless source of general-interest information and content including videos and music.

One drawback to our interconnectedness is that information offered on the Internet is uncensored and unverified—a virtual "Wild West" of data access. The Internet hosts unlimited material from innumerable electronic bulletin boards, Web sites, and publications, crisscrossing cultures and delivering ideas and data to consumers who may or may not exercise critical discernment. On the other hand, think of the criticism leveled against Yahoo, Microsoft, Google, and Cisco when they helped the Chinese government to monitor and censor content available to China's 100-plus million Internet users. Should the Internet be subject to censorship? Just as in the field of art, after years of debate we still wrestle with the issue of government censorship of material that lacks conformity with political agendas. According to Barry Steinhardt, director of the ACLU's Program on Technology and Liberty, "At stake are three basic civil liberties values: free speech, including access to information; privacy; and equality."[1]

Another potential drawback lies in our dependence on computers in contemporary public and private life; how they affect us both constructively and destructively has yet to be fully understood. We don't know the impact electronic media have on an individual's mindset. Those raised under the notion that they're free to ask their own questions don't realize that the very medium dictates the questions asked and, therefore, the knowledge retrieved.

Education in the Information Age plays a major role in structuring and defining elements of expanding cultural and economic globalization. In all academic disciplines, education now focuses on students' potential earning power. The high cost of obtaining a degree pressures students to finish their programs in the shortest time possible. This in turn deprives them of the opportunity to explore fields related to other interests, thereby curtailing their joy of learning for learning's sake, and consequently limiting creative growth.

The business model that saturates educational policies has also infiltrated other areas of cultural expression. Traditional boundaries between art, advertising, and entertainment are obsolete. Commercial artists utilize postmodernistic and pop culture styles, responding to the market in order to maximize profits. However, as their predecessors have done for centuries, independent artists more often than not use their creative expressions to interpret where societies are today and where they are headed, paying no heed to either public acceptance or the monetary value of their work.

An examination of trends in postmodern art provides a reading of the nutritional value of the multicultural menu we are offered. In trying to digest what we're looking at, we may not immediately understand what postmodern artists communicate. Simply addressing the visual aspects of their creations is not enough; we also need to examine the context, that is, artists' motivating force and the cultural environment that inspires them to create, if we're to understand the direction artists are pointing regarding our collective future.

This final chapter will end with a discussion of hunger, be it for food, material comfort, or spiritual guidance. Though hunger is the common thread, the disparity in ability to satisfy these types of hunger leads to alienation and separation among people as well as nations. Only after we recognize that our culture-specific code of ethics isn't always applicable to other contexts or cultures, and only after we've arrived at a consensus regarding ethical standards, will we be freed from the moral dilemmas presented by the means we currently employ to satisfy hunger. Not until we comprehend the interdependence between people of all nations, which paves the road to globalization, can we fully engage in alleviating the physical and/or emotional hunger that people of all nations are prone to suffer. Our survival depends on a new and universally acceptable ethical code that allows all to meet their needs, rather than exploiting those needs in order to scratch some imperialistic itch. Hopefully, this code will evolve to encompass an ethos transcending our current market-driven, self-serving, materialistic pursuits, leaving us better positioned to meet the uncertain future of our rapidly evolving global community.

Tracking Cultural Shifts

The burden of witnessing the conflict inherent to a world in flux rests heavily on the empathetic souls who can't close their eyes to it. They're the ones who share the hope and misery of all people affected by events throughout the world. Day and night, news is processed electronically and transmitted everywhere by satellite. Images and commentaries in the media regarding obesity in economically privileged societies, juxtaposed with reports of starvation in economically depressed societies, present vivid examples of paying the price of having too much or suffering the consequences of having too little. It's nearly impossible to become sensitive to international issues and events and remain indifferent to their impact on people without it haunting our private space and spiritual well-being. Do we answer the calls for help by sharing our capacity to generate wealth, or do we give in to "compassion fatigue" and tune them out? In the Information Age we're constantly updated with the effects of our responses to the challenges of our time.

Cultures, just like people, change over time, some faster than others. For example, Western cultures over the last 50 years have experienced drastic social changes that continue to escalate with each passing year. Some suggest that our knowledge bank doubles yearly. It's difficult to gauge whose lives have been impacted the most by new technology. Is it the shrinking rural population representing the most conservative segment, or is it the urbanites living a postmodern lifestyle with its accelerated rate of social change? Whether rural or urban, those most vulnerable to the debilitating effects of culture shock (or future shock) are the uneducated, the very young, the very old, and the immigrants—those among us who are either less prepared or overburdened with the instability and increasing rate of change.

Who pays attention to the destruction of traditional village infrastructure and the consequential disruption of lives? Do we really know the effects of cultural and economic globalization on developing countries?[2] Many of us in the United States have seen and felt the effects of job outsourcing—sooner or later, the current ideology of economic globalization, with its glorification of materialism, promises to penetrate every aspect of everyone's life. Rising economic standards clearly benefit those who share in them, but the costs shouldn't be ignored; namely, traditional lifestyles and values are endangered, and individuals are left with little choice in the matter. Environmental degradation is one such well-documented cost of globalization:

- In China, rapid industrialization has followed the pattern of the West, outstripping efforts to maintain clean air and water.
- In the Amazon Basin, the conversion of rain forest to over-grazed pasture land to supply the global beef industry has had drastic effects on micro- and macroclimates.
- From oil to minerals and diamonds, extraction industries have poisoned land, water, and politics, with no end in sight.

The above examples are but a few that clearly identify cultural shifts in attitude toward the natural environment, which have fluctuated between worshipping and respecting it, and dominating and destroying it.[3] The global nature of these attitude shifts became more pronounced in the late 20th century with climatologists' dire predictions of the effects of global warming, leading former US vice president and 2007 Nobel Peace Prize

Laureate Al Gore to warn, "We are witnessing a collision between our civilization and the Earth."[4]

We can readily identify the dismantling and transformation of past values in the visual arts, but making sense of the fragmented images coming at us ever faster through the media can be more difficult. Throw computers into the mix, and the challenge of tracking shifts in traditional world views becomes truly mind-boggling.

Living in the Digital Age

Though computers are central to modern life, vital to the functioning of everything from traffic lights to refrigerators to children's toys, it's perhaps the personal computer that has had the most profound impact on social interaction, blurring the line between private and public life. To a growing extent personal computers define how we conduct our lives.

The digital world is extraordinarily democratic; computers allow people who otherwise would be geographically or intellectually isolated to participate in vast social networks. Another culturally important aspect is the ability to use the computer as frequently or infrequently as desired. For those with access, the Internet serves as a great equalizer, disregarding the user's age, economic status, and location. Yet, as much as the computer provides a marginalized population with a new path to power, a widening gap in educational and economic opportunity known as the "digital divide" further marginalizes those left out of the digital revolution.[5]

Many seniors experience fear, frustration, and anger with society's increasing dependence on computers, perceiving them as non-human interlocutors that control their lives. Entering the Digital Age with this attitude, seniors refuse to learn about the wondrous capabilities of computers. Some humble themselves and even enjoy being taught by their grandchildren, while others prefer not to expose their ignorance. The technology that children seem to absorb like mother's milk can be very intimidating for seniors, who've survived far worse than having to learn the unfamiliar logic and new vocabulary involved in operating personal computers.

For seniors who've braved learning to use a computer, however, e-mail is a fabulous tool. Its importance can't be overstated, since keeping in regular contact with friends is good for the general well-being. Medical research shows that computer engagement can revitalize the brain and delay Alzheimer's disease, and e-mail is far more useful than the telephone for those who've suffered hearing loss. An added benefit is that it allows time for reflection, as dialogue need not be hurried.

When people become computer literate they can participate more actively in social and political life. During the Kashmiri conflict when India threatened to use nuclear power against Pakistan, millions of civilians who honor Gandhi's tradition of non-violence sent e-mails to the *Lok Sabha* (the directly elected branch of the Indian Parliament), pleading with the government to seek a peaceful solution through diplomatic means. This example illustrates how the Internet can empower citizens and impact political decisions in the authentic democratic tradition.

Technology transcends all borders, influencing all aspects of public and private domains. Our world's extreme dependency on computers was vividly illustrated at the dawn of the 21st century, when we held our collective breath at midnight, fearing that Y2K could wreak havoc by shutting down computers and disrupting entire nations' infrastructures. This of course didn't materialize, but it's a striking example of the global extent of our computer dependency.

Computers have the ability to satisfy innumerable cravings—curiosity, discovery, education, entertainment. The marvelous ability to address global audiences online and in real time, directly and intimately, is truly exhilarating. Computers give users the power of emotional freedom from the impositions of others. In face-to-face interactions, when we find ourselves caught in a banal conversation, it's difficult to remove ourselves gracefully; we're a captive audience. With computers we can choose anonymity and escape without explanation.

On the other hand this anonymity, together with the lack of censuring mechanisms, is open to abuse by imposters. Online dating can place participants in a dangerous position, and the bullying and retaliation that goes on in online social networks can be emotionally devastating for the young and vulnerable, even leading to suicide. Another growing problem is cyber crime, whose practitioners find ample opportunity to hone their skills, from hacking (stealing data from other people's computers) to phishing (sending scam e-mails that elicit confidential information).[6]

Computer addiction can also become problematic for users. Individuals who are unable to stop surfing the net for hours or even days on end have been labeled "mouse-potatoes." Computers can be so compelling that they become surrogates for live humans. When it comes to homelife, computers threaten to become one of the family's worst enemies, as they compete for time and attention. In addition to asocial behavior and withdrawal, computer addiction can lead to divorce resulting from neglected familial obligations. Parents worry about children who'd rather spend playtime on the computer than outdoors. For anyone, a prolonged sedentary lifestyle is unhealthy, often leading to obesity.[7]

Similar benefits and risks are associated with the proliferation of digital handheld devices. Many schools prohibit students from bringing cell phones, Walkmans, iPods, MP3 players, and Game Boys to school. The public at large is engaged in an ongoing dialogue regarding etiquette and safety in the use of cell phones in public places, especially behind the wheel of a moving vehicle. Yet the utility of cell phones in the realm of public safety and personal digital assistants in the business world is proven daily. The convergence of wireless communications and the Internet continues to spur the development of innovative uses.

The Internet links countless wireline and wireless communications networks, both public and private, tying the entire world together. It's a stimulating place in which to operate, because a user can choose whether to remain an observer or become an interactive participant.[8] Participation isn't limited to blogging or instant messaging—the growth of commercial Web sites is phenomenal. Virtual and brick-and-mortar realities meet at online stores and auctions, made all the more real with a click of the "buy now" button that brings a real package to our door.

In virtual reality, users create an environment unencumbered by physical limitations. We can go anywhere, be anyone, and do anything we desire. The very first experiments with virtual reality were crude at best. Though the depiction of human beings at first had the appearance of being computer-generated, programmers are now able to digitally manipulate photography and videography to create lifelike images nearly indistinguishable from our natural environment, contributing to a dreamlike, altered reality.

Virtual reality technologies are driving astounding advancements in simulation applications for training, gaming, design, and business and social networking. Technology today can accommodate just about anything the mind can imagine. Innovative architectural structures, such as Frank Gehry's Disney Concert Hall in Los Angles, would be unthinkable without computer-aided design software.[9]

So far the biggest hits in the software market are found in the gaming sector and revolve around themes of sex and violence. The effects of violence in digital gaming have yet to be determined; some studies find no demonstrable correlation, while others claim that video games foster real-life enactments. Studies in Japan seem to indicate that screen violence has little if any effect on street violence there. In Japan such video games are enormously popular; however Japan also has one of the lowest crime rates in the world. This is perhaps a prime example of how we must consider cultural context in examining such questions.

But virtual reality supports much more than sex and violence. It's also become a significant avenue for the creativity of younger artists, for example, Projekt30's virtual gallery, "A Glass Darkly."[10] This show reaches out to a number of artists the world over, inviting them to use traditional or digital media and post their works for the review of the Internet audience. The exhibitions are structured as competitions, borrowing from reality TV shows inasmuch as they invite the public to be the jury. This has several revolutionary consequences:

- Validation and interpretation of art is extended beyond the privileged theoreticians and placed in the hands of the common viewers.
- Visitors are free to contact the artists for feedback and comments.
- The public has the opportunity to enter a creative partnership with artists.
- Artists can experience the joy and sorrow associated with receiving public feedback on their work.

By engaging such a large portion of the public in their respective ventures, artists and virtual galleries share the future of marketing research with professional advertising agencies and political advisors. Here too we acknowledge the necessity of bridging the digital divide in order to extend interactivity to every member of the global community.

Educating Toward Integration and Cultural Globalization

Indhira Gandhi, India's first female prime minister (1966-1977, 1980-1984), ran her election on the ambitious political platform of "*Garibi Hatao!*" (remove poverty). Her campaign mantra has since become an international priority. At best, this means funding projects that will build successful, functioning, sustainable economies in poor countries across the globe. It means educating the world's people who've yet to take part in the positive interdependence envisioned for the Global Era. A billion people in this world are illiterate, and 120 million children don't go to school. But we know that every year of schooling adds 10 to 15 percent a year to the income of people in poor countries for the rest of their lives. Eradicating poverty will not only increase their productivity and quality of life, but it will also increase their longevity. *The World Almanac and Book of Facts 2008* shows the correlation between life expectancy of people living in rich and poor nations: In most Western European and Scandinavian countries, women have an average life expectancy of 82-plus years, outliving men by 4 to 8 years, whereas in many African countries life expectancy for men and women is less than 40 years.

A globalization of education is underway, and academic institutions are addressing the need for education in the fight against poverty. Long Beach, California, which markets itself as the International City, is a multicultural community with approximately half a million people of various origins: 36 percent Hispanic, 33 percent White, 15 percent Black, and 12 percent Asian. With many ethnic groups speaking different languages, educational excellence is difficult to achieve. One of the problems is that the very program that aspired to narrow the achievement gap between higher-income Caucasian students and lower-income non-Caucasian students—the No Child Left Behind Act of 2001—at the same time pursues the idealistic policy of treating every student the same. These are incompatible pursuits, since clearly students who have to acquire proficiency in the English language, or those with less preparation in intellectual discourse, need more preparation to compete academically with students who come from homes where discussion and exchange of ideas, in English, is part of the dinnertime ritual.

When the California State University system launched a step-by-step program to help middle and high school students prepare for college, the program's "How to Get to College" poster was originally released in English and Spanish. Five years later, the poster was also printed in Korean, Chinese, and Vietnamese, recognizing the need to reach the growing diversity of minorities.[11] The irony is, of course, that English is the language students need to be proficient in if they are to succeed at the university. But the example presents an interesting dilemma, since in spite of the recognition of diversity, the underlying assumption is that all students enter these educational institutions on equal footing.

Let's take a look at the vision statement for Long Beach City College in California:

> Long Beach City College prepares students to be successful in the world of the 21st century. Sitting at a global crossroads, the college constantly crafts its educational programs to meet the needs of students living in
>
> - a world of increased complexity and speed
> - a world both global and remarkably accessible
> - a world technologically advanced but intensely interdependent.
>
> A culturally diverse college, Long Beach City College welcomes all people who desire to grow and serve. The college nurtures a vibrant environment that cultivates a passion for learning, which continues for life.[12]

With the current state of affairs, this idealism places the burden on the faculty to balance lofty goals with realistic performance objectives. The process will take much patience, skill, and time to accomplish. A more realistic solution would be to expand remedial education so that students have a better opportunity to attain the competencies required to succeed in higher education.

Colleges and universities in the USA are notoriously expensive to attend. In response to spiraling costs, universities are experimenting with business models, the goals being cost reduction and increased efficiency. For many students, a large part of their economic hardship is the high cost of textbooks. Certainly, students in the USA know this problem well, and it's magnified for students in developing countries.

Counteracting this problem is a US-based initiative to make new textbooks downloadable, free of charge, from the Internet. The objective is to produce about a thousand texts covering biology, physics, mathematics, and chemistry. Each title would be supported by corporate sponsorship, and professors from around the world have been invited to contribute to this effort. An advantage to Internet publishing is the ease of updating material at low cost. The books will be written in English and translated by volunteers into other languages. Another innovative facet of this initiative is that students will be invited to actively participate in a wiki-based program to contribute to the ongoing revisions. For the first time, these continuing revisions will put current texts in the hands of all, including students from developing countries. An advisory board drawn from universities in Colombia, Egypt, Malaysia, South Africa, Uganda, and the United Kingdom has been set up to oversee the books' creation.[13]

Computer-based distance learning facilitates transnational education, a central tool for developing global multiculturalism. Through the power of the Internet, we can bring education to more people faster than by other more traditional means. In 1997 networking provider Cisco Systems established a public-private partnership called the Cisco Networking Academy Program, which in its first decade delivered technical training to more than 232,000 students and 8,000 educational institutions in 133 countries including Bangladesh, Cambodia, Mali, Chad, and the Congo.

Online content can be used in a variety of ways: it can provide primary or supplemental curriculum in a traditional classroom setting, it can be administered and taught entirely over the Internet (distance learning), or it can straddle both environments (flex learning). Of course, standardizing global online content requires cultural awareness and sensitivity, especially in the arts, humanities, and social sciences, areas where content can clash with local traditions and laws.

As countries grow closer politically, economically, and intellectually through the use of high-tech communications systems, is it reasonable to expect that they'll be able to retain their distinct cultural characteristics? Some see in globalization the threat of cultural homogenization or "gray-out," and they shudder at the idea.[14] Others see globalization as positive, inevitably resulting in greater affluence. While there is probably some truth to both of these views, the degree of interdependence originating with trade agreements and economics influences all branches of cultural expression; its extent varies in accordance with individual countries' commitment to modernization. In the words of former US president Bill Clinton, "...the great mission of the 21st century world is to make it a genuine global community. To move from mere interdependence to integration, to a community that has three characteristics: shared responsibilities, shared benefits, and shared values."[15] Obviously the shared values Clinton mentions presuppose a shared system of humanistic ethics.

As we've discussed above, religious belief systems belong to cultures' primary core concepts. Whereas individual interests frequently supersede the welfare of the collective, religion has traditionally served as a cultural vehicle for ethical codes designed to keep individual interests in check. People living in traditional, conservative societies tend to be committed to institutional religions, but in many cultures modernization has meant a move toward secularism and away from institutional religion. In Cologne, Germany, for example, three architectural structures that stand side by side, a cathedral, a museum, and a railway station, historically had served three different functions, but as Jack Flam notes, their functions have shifted: "These days, cathedrals are becoming museums, and museums are becoming railway stations."[16]

Amidst the materialistic aspirations and hectic day-to-day living that characterize modern societies, many people still acknowledge an ethic inspired by trust in human decency. Some regard this ethic as the "Golden Rule," some might call it secular humanism, and others don't bother with a label, but an old German expression exemplifies the general trend: "*Fürchte Gott, tue Recht, scheue niemand*" (Fear God, do right, harm no one.) You hear the expression to this day in Germany, although the God-fearing part has largely been dropped.

While conservative religious leaders warn parishioners of the godlessness of secular humanism, their more progressive counterparts are looking to welcome positive moral values regardless of the source of inspiration. In September 2006 the Faculty of Religious Studies at McGill

University in Montreal sponsored "World's Religions after September 11: A Global Congress." The first task of the congress was to draft the *Universal Declaration of Human Rights by the World's Religions*. In the words of McGill Professor Arvind Sharma, "If all the religions of the world come together to prepare this declaration, in this sense the gap between the secular and the religious can be breached."[17]

Obviously, peaceful coexistence is more likely under a widely accepted umbrella ethic. The effort to arrive at such a macro ethic has won the support of four Nobel Peace Laureates—the Dalai Lama, Archbishop Desmond Tutu of South Africa, Bishop Carlos Belo of East Timor, and Madame Shirin Ebadi of Iran—as well as the Council for a Parliament of World's Religions, and human rights champions from a broad spectrum of nationalities and professions.

The creation of a universally viable ethic—marrying the life-confirming morals of a myriad of religious and secular ideals, and divorcing the moral degradation of excessive sectarianism—is an enormous undertaking. The draft is under constant revision,[18] as it is difficult to reconcile fundamental stereotypical views of Western cultures as committed to advancing physical comfort and materialism, and of Eastern cultures presumably more concerned with spirituality and modernizing "without becoming a mere clone of the West."[19]

An ethic we can all aspire to and live with, one that doesn't require the sacrifice of anyone's cultural integrity, must address yet another type of religion: national identity. Patriotism, like religion, is something to be greatly honored when it inspires moral behavior, and greatly feared otherwise. Of the many reasons humans have cited in extinguishing the lives of other humans, patriotism rates right up there with sectarianism. On the other hand, if Homo sapiens can hope to coexist within a circle of multiple religions, we can still hold out hope for coexisting on a globe of multiple nations. Multinational passports and citizenship are the patriotic equivalent to secular humanism, in that they provide for multinational coexistence, rather than precluding it.

After World War I, the Norwegian explorer and 1922 Nobel Peace Prize Laureate Fridtjof Nansen instituted what became known as the international passport. This passport was recognized by sixty countries and helped millions of refugees relocate. In an ongoing effort to build on the lessons learned from the devastation of centuries of warfare in Europe, the

European Union (EU) introduced a passport valid for all citizens of its soon to be 30 member states.[20]

Globalization now provides us with a bounty of cultural discourse and limitless possibilities for multiple identifications. Here, we're able to transcend cultural and geographical specificities by tapping into the geography of the mind as we acknowledge that the products of our material culture are composed of universal elements. Artists are good at focusing on common frames of reference, but they're pretty useless, as history has demonstrated, when we can't extend our common frames of reference beyond the primary core concepts that we grew up with but others didn't.

Tracking Visual Culture in a Postmodern World

Visual culture is the most prominent among postmodern expressions, and multicultural visual literacy is of particular importance today, because we live in a multicultural society whose ties to other cultures are becoming increasingly interdependent. Many of us don't share the same spoken language; consequently, the visual media continue to grow in popularity as means of multicultural communication.

A characteristic typical of the postmodern multicultural visual movement is the tendency to blur distinctions between traditional disciplines. Creativity is no longer defined by the ability to work flexibly within set boundaries, but rather as an ability to question boundaries and push beyond perceived limits. Interdisciplinary approaches squeeze multimedia, entertainment, and advertising, as well as what was once considered highbrow and lowbrow art, all together onto the same palette. Creators of postmodern culture and fine artists express their particular philosophies in their chosen identities as global citizens.

Advertising is the child resulting from the three-way marriage of art, technology, and capitalism. We encounter its fantastic imagery everywhere: at home on TV and the Internet, in storefront windows, and on roadside billboards. Nobody escapes the effects of advertising. Research has shown that even three-year-old children are not immune to advertisements. In an experiment, children preferred carrots placed on a McDonald's French fries bag to carrots served without the McDonald's logo.[21]

In principle, advertising is one of the contemporary media in which we can register creativity completely free of ethics. For example, Mona Lisa, her subtle smile intact, is perceived as seductive when used for advertising birth control, forever robbing her of her original, otherworldly artistic expression. Nothing is sacred any more. Advertisers are recycling works of art from all cultures, even with themes from religious art, by changing context and intent for the sake of marketing consumer goods.

Another attention-getting device is to irritate viewers by having them look in vain for what the selling product might be in a stunning visual presentation. Mass culture becomes a mere marketing vehicle for large corporations. Anyone who has visited Disneyland, Hollywood, or Las Vegas has also experienced the homogeneous and escapist qualities of these destinations. By its 50th anniversary, The Walt Disney Company had opened theme parks in Florida, Paris, Tokyo, and Hong Kong. In these theme parks visitors can buy into and briefly indulge their fantasies of "the happiest place on earth," as well as dream about the marvels of space culture and its future. These recreational facilities gave rise to the "Americanization" of culture, a concept that on the one hand is perceived as cultural contamination, or as a threat to the survival of other cultures, but on the other hand has been embraced, reformulated, and imbued with new local definitions. According to a recent visitor, even in remote Tibet, "Lhasa is transforming into a Chinese version of the capitalist Wild West, with karaoke bars and Disney-like Buddhist theme parks."[22]

Mickey Mouse and other Disney memorabilia are sold all over the world. While kitsch may outlast junk food, they belong in the same category in that both are readily available in public venues, and both feed and briefly satisfy impulse buying. In many ways this global commercialism is like a cultural Esperanto, a language constructed by pulling eclectically from past and present languages. Eclecticism is one of the most defining characteristics of Postmodernism.

Theme parks and resorts appeal to people of all ages. Another major American innovation and component of mass culture targets the younger generation in particular: MTV's powerful message is broadcast throughout the world. Artistically, MTV programming is one of the most original voices of contemporary urban pop culture; as a result this branch of popular culture courts aggression, violence, and sex. Since youths account for the largest percentages of the human population, particularly in

Asian and in Third World countries, their preferences are pervasive in today's visual mass culture.

MTV's strong grip on audiences can be explained by its use of synesthesia, defined as the confluence of several perceptual faculties that, in the case of MTV, result in an intense seduction of consciousness. Free of linear narratives, MTV's imagery is all the more powerful because it synthesizes several forms of expression. True to its postmodern style, MTV ignores artistic boundaries by meshing instrumental and vocal music with visuals—dancing, acting, and imagery. This medium has technique and artistry working in tandem; the marriage of multiple media is the message, and the message throbs with violence, sex, and greed. Two representative superstars of MTV, Madonna and Michael Jackson, have led public and private lives that are outstanding examples of postmodernist ethics enacted. With no apparent structure, story line, or narrative, and with shifting focus, MTV programming pulsates with energy and pounding rhythms, infused with great beauty and pathos, all in the service of marketing. This duality of expression and purpose is typical of Postmodernism.

Professional reviewers and the public who question the quality of postmodern art must still realize that their evaluation criteria are irrelevant. With impudence, postmodern artists appropriate, recycle, and subject masterpieces of any culture or period to a rebirthing through the processes of deconstruction. Recycling known masterpieces of the past or placing familiar objects in unconventional settings serves a dual purpose: it entices the viewer by using the familiar as an entry point, feeding on the curiosity to explore the new statement; it also serves as a reminder that the meaning of the familiar can change with the context.

Viewers will likely be reminded of the original work that in the hands of a postmodern artist has been transformed to a provocative re-creation. The artist in turn anticipates an audience response ranging from rejection, to anger, to impatience and curiosity—a response driven by the need to understand the message. Though to be understood by the public is important for the artists' road to recognition and fame, most artists continue to create as they wish—whether or not the public understands their art—distancing themselves from public interpretations of what their art might mean or will come to mean.

Artists participate in various international exhibitions that regularly open in capitals around the world, where they offer their works "to whom it may concern" in the global market. They don't seek out their audience; the audience seeks out the art and brings to these exhibitions their own backgrounds, cultures, and agendas. Often there's as much emphasis placed on who is doing the seeing as on what there is to see. A study of the attendees would identify other artists as the most faithful visitors. Artists today are like professionals in any field—they're experts who communicate most easily with colleagues within their own profession.

Exhibitors most likely subscribe to a modern, urban lifestyle. Their creations are similarly removed from nature; their artistic vocabulary responds to the ocular reality of the inorganic urban environment. Their canvases are large, frequently abstract, fragmented, and dehumanized. If humans are depicted, they may be deformed or computer-generated abstracts. Stylistically speaking, the aesthetics of computer-rendered postmodern art closely parallels the aesthetics of contemporary lifestyles in the megalopolis: both highlight and glorify the fast-paced, impersonal urban tempo. If anything, they pose questions, but don't answer them.

While some elements, such as experimentation and the cult of the new, remain from the early 20th-century Modernism art movement, an obvious difference lies in profound changes in the postmodern artists' emphasis on the purpose of art. Most interesting is postmodern art's function to awaken viewers to the unpredictable and uncontrollable nature of medical and scientific discoveries. One such artist is Wang Du, born in 1956 in Wuhan, China. He immigrated to Paris in 1990 and married a French journalist. Wang Du is known as an iconoclast who sculpts and paints three-dimensional objects from his daily life in Paris. In a 1997 exhibition that featured sculptures of nudes, Wang explained that "the people of the future [will] enjoy the ability, through biotechnology, to redesign their bodies as they choose." Much of his work focuses on the relationship between the media and public consciousness, and the artificial manipulations imposed by the two. In connection with an exhibition called "Disposable Reality" (2000) he said, "I organize my projects just like the media do with reality."[23]

Postmodern art is seen as commentaries of reality in flux and not intended to last, created for the here and the now, or as a forecast of the future. Swiss-born artist Jean Tinguely (1925-1991) is best known for building whimsical self-destructing contraptions out of scraps. His *Homage to New York* (1960) challenges the notion of static art.

Postmodernism fosters an attitude of rebellion against present and past cultures. Its producers represent a consciousness-raising group, challenging the status quo much as the Dadaist artists did before them.[24] Dadaist philosophy expressed despondency and nihilism, having lost faith in humankind after the experiences of World War I. Postmodern artists, no matter what their medium, present a deconstructed, fragmented reality. In spite of the fact that most of their art is amoral in its message, they're not trying to impose their personal views on the viewers; rather, their vision of chaos is created for the purpose of changing the public's attitude, inviting them to enter a discourse about the envisioned enormity of an unknown future.

As provocateurs, postmodern artists view themselves as messengers with the intent to

- provoke by taking viewers outside their comfort zone
- challenge viewers to accept that which is not understandable
- understand that nothing is normal, and nothing impossible
- encourage viewers to trust and explore the unknown aspects of human existence
- help viewers cope with and meet change without fear
- dare viewers to face chaos without losing their minds and self-control.

Artists are no longer primarily in the service of a given sponsor or public. Who are they then? This is a question that individuals in search of a definitive answer find troublesome. The following definitions of artists and their status in society were proposed in 1980 by the United Nations Educational, Scientific and Cultural Organization (UNESCO):

1. Artist is taken to mean any person who creates or gives creative expression to, or re-creates works of art, who considers his artistic creation to be an essential part of his life, who contributes in this

way to the development of art and culture and who is or asks to be recognized as an artist, whether or not he is bound by any relations of employment or association.

2. The word status signifies, on the one hand, the regard accorded to artists, defined as above, in a society, on the basis of the importance attributed to the part they are called upon to play therein and, on the other hand, recognition of the liberties and rights, including moral, economic and social rights, with particular reference to income and social security, which artists should enjoy.[25]

Who are artists? Artists are self-proclaimed poets and prophets, continually reinventing themselves, and us with them. Since postmodern artists envision a global audience, they are at times even willing to explain what their art is about. Fredric Jameson sees artists in "a situation faced by post-modernity in general, and to which its artists and subjects are obliged to respond in a variety of ways." This situation, which Jameson posits as "the end of temporality," is characterized by the "shrinkage of existential time and the reduction to a present that hardly qualifies as such any longer, given the virtual effacement of that past and future that can alone define a present in the first place."[26]

Artists, while possessing pronounced emotional sensitivity, are subservient to a creative prowess that rests on the artists' ability to integrate emotions with ideas. With or without formal training, artists intuit the existential threat of an invasion of a technocratic society with its persistent artificial spaces and virtual realities. Artists are therefore in a unique position to help us, their viewers, internalize and cope with today's changing realities. Exposure to art can ease our paralytic responses to culture shock and isolation. By responding to metaphors for feelings and bicultural or multicultural identities, we viewers can recontextualize art in all of its shifting shapes and use it to change our own habits of consciousness.

Artists capitalize on internal and external conflicts, hinting at the shape of tomorrow. Who owns the future? We can't know to what extent artists and their work will effect tomorrow's policies, but if the past is any indication, even the current "end of temporality" won't put an end to our capacity for recontextualization.

Coping as Global Citizens

The global citizen is a product of the geography of the mind. Coping with the unknown requires each member of this mind space to behave responsibly. Superpowers of the world need to be especially sensitive to the leadership roles they play, taking care not to overpower smaller nations economically or culturally. In our desire to create a global culture, it's imperative that we remember the difference between melting pots and salad bowls and tapestries. Cultural literacy should never mask the designs of cultural imperialism.

Up to this point we've used the USA as an example of a superpower and as a platform for multicultural understanding. As such, the USA shouldn't be viewed in isolation. The challenges we all face in our reach for higher living standards are similar throughout the world. The first point on the multicultural learning curve occurs where two people from divergent cultures meet, ideally resulting in the development of a mutual, bicultural relationship. Multiculturalism pertaining to peaceful cohabitation of various ethnic groups is the next point. Cultural globalization is an organic process that takes time; it follows a pattern of expansion, starting with individuals who embrace successively larger numbers of people from any number of cultures. Fueling this growth is the ever-expanding influence of mass communication and global networking. Global consciousness is a concept cementing our interconnectedness. Our species' scientific name, *Homo sapiens*—"wise humans"—reminds us of our obligation to act with wisdom as we connect with other cultures.

As already mentioned, the first of many tasks facing our future world community is to eradicate poverty and hunger of all kinds. The effects of biological hunger, often not fully realized by the affected individual, debilitate both body and mind. Psychological hunger produces feelings of restlessness and despair. The common denominators of the two frequently lead to aggression and acts of violence, which can only be alleviated through a more equitable distribution of resources. War and poverty are intrinsically tied together.

The Hunger Site estimates that one billion people in the world suffer from hunger and malnutrition.[27] Past experiences based on assisting developing countries have shown the need to find new, creative ways to help. The simple act of giving without further commitment and human interaction has proved ineffective, as it places the receiving community or nation in a position of inferiority. The modern concept of "help to self-help" renders the older model obsolete. As a Chinese saying goes, "If you want to help a man do not give him a fish, but teach him how to fish."

A significant new approach in giving was created by Muhammad Yunus, who was awarded the Nobel Peace Prize in 2006 for his Grameen Bank Project. A citizen of a nation suffering deprived economic conditions with an average yearly income per person of less $1,770, Yunus introduced a program to combat poverty based on personal experiences with the problems facing Bangladesh. The program addresses poverty at its grassroots level and gets rid of most of the administrative paperwork and financial drain involved in traditional money lending. Yunus' "micro financing" model grants small, low-interest loans to Bangladeshi village women. Many variations of financing Third World entrepreneurial projects have been inspired by Yunus' operating formula, benefiting the poorest of the poor. Repayment rates have exceeded expectations (about 97 percent) and are arranged so that a person who has benefitted from the program can then lend money to another in the community. Such informal economic assistance enables products to be sold on the local market, and the economic gains remain within the village to promote the general welfare of the village.[28]

Offering an alternative to loan sharks who exploit the poor is an important step. Desperate circumstances are too easily abused by unethical lenders who profit from high-interest loans in perpetuity, especially in developing countries. In China for example, a huge number of internal migrants moving from rural communities to the cities are made up of farmers and merchants whose families are driven into bankruptcy by a debt that continues to grow year by year.

Other challenges facing developing nations are familiar to post-industrial societies, such as problems associated with industrialization including urban sprawl, stress on resources, and environmental degradation. A case in point again is Bangladesh, a country the size of Texas with a population of over 140 million. In the last three decades, the capital city of Dacca has grown from 1 million to more than 12 million inhabitants. The loss of agricultural land to sprawling megalopolises the world over is of grave concern. Furthermore, scientists predict diminishing fresh water supplies due to global warming, which could increase the size of the world's population living without access to potable water (currently 1/6).[29]

It's obligatory that we take our stewardship of the earth seriously. Still, many accept that at this point environmental protection standards cannot be universally adopted. How can we expect the starving masses to be concerned about long-term consequences of the continuing destruction of the environment when a much more immediate problem lies in their quest of simple day-to-day survival? The deforestation of the Amazon Basin highlights the plight of struggling farmers whose means of livelihood are causing environmental damage. Here, however, is a poignant example of our interconnectedness, for this ecosystem's natural resources, so crucial to the earth's collective health, can benefit from the international community's shared educational and technological resources to bring sustainable agricultural methods to the region. An adequate level of nutrition unleashes creative energies that free people up to think and act about concerns beyond their immediate physical survival.

Addressing the disparity between the haves and have-nots is a prime example of situational ethics. Those whose talents lie in generating wealth must understand that their responsibility in the global community doesn't end with supplying jobs—until poverty has been minimized, the wealthy must acknowledge that their stewardship, as well as that of their workers, includes the health and welfare of every member of the global community. The challenge is first to assent to an ethic of fair distribution of resources, a program to which every nation and person will be committed, and second to secure its implementation.

Another major challenge we face in creating a global culture is the question of governmental control over the individual. For many cultures, privacy protection is an alien concept. In most Western cultures, however, we balk at the prospect of Big Brother making our private lives and thoughts public property. Yet even Western governments regulate many aspects of people's lives. In the USA, so-called "nanny-bills" mandate personal protection, such as wearing seat belts and motorcycle helmets. While many view such measures as sensible, others perceive these laws as over-regulated intrusions into their private lives, curtailing individual freedom.

Technology designed to enhance consumer safety and security while driving could just as easily serve a government's perceived need to more effectively surveil its citizens. For example, many late-model cars come equipped with microprocessors that function as event data recorders (EDRs), commonly referred to as "black boxes," which can be used to monitor driving behavior in employees, car renters, or teenage drivers. EDRs track location, speed, and mileage, and provide accurate and detailed records in case of accident or theft. Additional personal information can be encoded in the magnetic strip on the back of the driver's license itself.

Internet services allow parents to track their children through Global Positioning System (GPS) microchips embedded in cell phones or pendants worn around the neck, or even implanted beneath the skin. Parolees can similarly be monitored through ankle bracelets. Aversion to this degree of private and/or public oversight is voiced by privacy advocates who consider central databases invasive and the potential for abuse threatening.[30]

Internet-based social network users assume that their entries are private information, yet because of the very public nature of the Internet, potential employers and schools can go online to glean personal data about perspective employees and students. The assumption that the discussion between bloggers and their public is confidential is fallacious, and the broadcasting of a very public exchange of opinions blurs the lines between what was once highly private and personal, and what is now very public.

Might we be overrating the value of privacy? The right of privacy is a byproduct of the uniquely Western concept of individualism. Is it our just reward that another uniquely Western institution, the corporation, seems to be redefining our concept of privacy for us, with its market research practices of data mining our behaviors, charting our tastes, and predicating our needs?

Science fiction writers of the 20th century foretold of a centralization of power and a population connected to a global computer—technology-driven *E pluribus unum*! Now as we survey our 21st-century surroundings we find that the future is here, and what's left of our private domain is shrinking. Perhaps we need to rethink what ought to be private, if anything, since we all share the same roles as mothers, fathers, daughters, sons, employers, employees, and citizens. In recognizing our inherent commonality, it's our responsibility to redefine our individuality in spite of the fear of drowning as our private lives become increasingly public.

In the previous pages, we've stopped just short of calling for a complete and utter conceptual transformation as the only path of escaping the boundaries of the self. The concept of otherness is contagious; as soon as we create others in our minds, we ourselves create an otherness in the minds of others. On the one hand the concept of otherness functions as an identifier that helps each group distinguish themselves; on the other hand fear of otherness causes alienation, creating a distance not only between us and others, but also between us and ourselves.

Perhaps the ability to embrace the other within ourselves lies closer than we might imagine. Octavio Paz, 1990 Nobel Literature Prize Laureate, posited the process of identifying with the other in this way:

The image transmutes man and converts him in turn into an image, that is, into a space where opposites fuse.... And man himself, split asunder since birth, is reconciled with himself when he becomes an image, when he becomes another.[31]

In the act of creation, artists experience the other as a self. By recontextualizing artists' creations, this act of empathy, of reconciling our self with the other, is open to us, the viewers, as well. When the lessons of Postmodernism have been internalized, Post Postmodernism—or whatever we end up calling the prevailing aesthetic of the coming era—will follow in natural progression. What will that era look like? We're deciding right now, whether by default, subconsciously, or with intent, consciously.

The great value that art holds for artists and viewers alike transcends the appreciation of beauty, edifying as that purpose is; art leads us to question the validity or truth of our perceptions. For example most of us are familiar with da Vinci's *Mona Lisa*, but how many have seen the actual painting? Seeing the actual painting for ourselves opens us up to three experiential levels: given the chance to see the original, people are often surprised by its diminutive size; the actual viewing then overrides the mental image, or our visualization of it before we experienced the original; finally, in recalling our actual viewing of the image, we further recontextualize the experience, and this memory updates the experience of seeing the image in person.

Therefore if we designate the mental or visualized image we had prior to experiencing the painting, A; and the actual experience, B; with C being the memory of the experience; I propose that B overrides A, and C overrides B. The same equation holds true when applied to culture.

A, B, and C differ inevitably for each individual, qualitatively and quantitatively, according to the individual viewer's mental horizon. Multiply these variations by our global population, and the experiential variations are as numerous and mind-boggling as the stars in our universe. This is the problem that postmodern artists address, whether subconsciously or consciously. By decoding their art, we gain proficiency in decoding cultures, their relativism, and their pluralism.

It's no longer necessary to travel abroad to experience other cultures; they come to us, invade us, and at times even seem to take over. It takes inner stamina to monitor the instability of our fluxing realities as we experience future and culture shock simultaneously. Following the lead of postmodern aesthetics, we probably won't find beauty in every traditional cultural value we come face-to-face with, but the process will help us create space in the landscape of our minds to accommodate the other. As more of us adopt an empathetic mindset, our global community will have far more beauty to offer than we would've imagined possible.

Our Western view of events occurring along a vertical axis has been replaced by the postmodern concept of a horizontal or lateral expanse. We feel stress when we perceive these intersecting boundaries as unacceptable—as transgressions rather than acceptable transitions. Training to overcome the construed divide between the *us* and *them*, that is, the otherness of *other*, without giving up our own identity, is a sound recipe for learning how to cope, banishing the primordial threat of *them,* and giving a truly inclusive meaning to *us*. We become as it were virtual immigrants in our inner landscapes. The demanding mental frames of reference inherent in real globalization constitute an expansion of the mind from the vertical axis of our personal roots to a lateral expansion, claiming the whole world, including the universe, as our own. We can no longer maintain the NIMBY ("not in my backyard") attitude, since we all share the same backyard with the same flowers and the same weeds. We've inherited a community garden in every sense; whether it flourishes or lies fallow is up to each of us gardeners tending our individual plots. We'll all fare better as more of us recognize our interdependence in the community.

Humility is the redeemer when we lack wisdom and don't know what to do. Education potentially gives us the courage to stop history from repeating itself. In the words of Israeli President Shimon Peres, "Knowledge applies to what has already taken place, while vision relates to what might be. It is science and technology which then converts creative ideas and potential solutions for global problems into a reality."[32]

In this book we've explored the importance of context and seen how the meaning of art is in constant flux according to the changing times and cultures in which it's created. Recognizing the interdependency of art and cultural literacy is the key to developing the emotional dexterity we'll all need to negotiate a global environment wound together ever more tightly by emerging technology. The success of our species could ultimately hinge on a wild card that we as yet understand very poorly: emotion.[33]

Can we in the end hope to educate our emotions? Can emotions be trained? Can we even be held responsible for our emotions? Answers to these questions remain to be seen.

Tomorrow's discoveries, especially those born of our research of inner and outer space, will further dramatize our incomprehensively large and precariously small place among infinite universes, exposing us to wrenching and powerful emotions. In the future, if we believe we can educate our emotions and direct them toward cultivating humility, love, and respect for life in all its manifestations, we may manage to create a much wiser use of "shock and awe."[34]

END

EPILOGUE

This book is a culmination of promises I made to myself as a child. During the German occupation of Norway, the war imposed many restrictions and difficulties in our lives. My family had evacuated from our home in Oslo to the summerhouse in the countryside. For several years we depended on miserly ration cards, and our freedom to move about was severely limited. When my sister became ill and needed to go to a hospital, we could not take her because we were unable to obtain the travel permit necessary for the four-hour train journey. Already feeling encaged, I crawled into the doghouse to hide, and I curled up and wept for a long time. Finally, afraid that my sister would die, I was enraged. It was then I swore that when the war ended and I grew up, I would let no one ever stop me from going anywhere again. I was going to see the world. My father, who had already worked for peace through his books and lectures, and in spite of the war, would not be silenced regarding his constant concern. The impact of our discussions impressed not only me, but also my brother and sister, who went on to become medical doctors serving in various countries throughout the world. The central question for all of us remains, what will it take for everyone to be able to live in peaceful coexistence?

My Norwegian father and Austrian mother were internationally renowned scholars in their respective fields, and they had exposed me to an interdisciplinary academic dialogue long before I'd considered its significance. My father, Anathon Aall, was a professor of philosophy and founded the Institute of Psychology at the University of Oslo. He lectured at the universities of Tokyo, Oxford, Harvard, Chicago, and Columbia, among others. In the post-World War I era, it had become clear to my father and many of his colleagues that a lack of communication between the sciences and humanities, disciplines that often seemed to work in direct opposition to one another, undercut the academy's enlightened promise of contributing to social progress.

In the 1920s, Dr. Aall began exchanging letters with scholars in various fields, seeking ideas, authors, editors, and funding to begin publication of an interdisciplinary journal to be called The International Review of Social Biology and Psychology. His position was that science, with its empirically documented facts, enjoyed immediate international validity, whereas the humanistic disciplines were intrinsically culturally enmeshed and, as a result, marginalized in contemporary academic discourse that spoke to the burgeoning social unrest of the period. My father was convinced that establishing an interdisciplinary dialogue among scholars from all over the world could serve as a critical international peace-building conduit.

In his outreach, Dr. Aall corresponded with many brilliant contemporaries, such as Franz Boas, Edward Thorndike, and Albert Einstein. Einstein himself responded with the following letter:

> November 19, 1927
> Professor Anathon Aall, Oslo
>
> Most Venerable Colleague!
>
> Your plan has my greatest sympathy, and I believe that the Committee on Intellectual Cooperation[1] is there to support you. This committee surely has knowledge-based insights to promote the goals that are important to the League of Nations. This of course must also include the question of race relations of which you are well aware.
>
> Respectfully yours,
> A. Einstein[2]

In spite of the considerable international interest and encouragement of colleagues, financing such a project remained a vexing problem. That said, in retrospect it is clear that there was no single reason why father's plan did not materialize. Perhaps it was partly the complication of logistics that accompanied my parents' marriage in 1928—only a few months after Father's communication with Einstein—and their subsequent guest lecturing at the University of Tokyo. The Stock Market Crash in 1929 and the resulting Great Depression provided challenges of their own. Then came the Second World War, which shattered the dreams of so many.

Today world peace remains illusive. As many times before, one man's life is not sufficient to complete such a far-reaching goal; rather, it falls to like-minded spirits to follow up. My emotional journey while writing this book brought me closer to my father's vision for the future of humanity. It is now my duty—my burden, at times—to share with others, his and my idealism of global peace. I hope my book will put you on that path.

Upon completing its writing, I came to realize that the issues in my book deal with the same pattern of problems that my father dedicated his life to address. The questions we face today are not different from those of the past. The primary issue, now as then, is a matter of orientation and attitude: economics, war, and the inability to deal with multiple perspectives brought to bear on those problems, all stand in the way of negotiations and solutions.

There is a difference between information and knowledge. Gandhi, the great peacemaker, advised, "Always know your opponents and always meet them halfway." The former demands our willingness to collect information, and the latter to use our human insight. Wisdom, in short, relates to experienced knowledge. Conflict resolution mandates that we consider not only a single point of view, but also multiple perspectives. The origin of our present dilemma is not merely a lack of knowledge, but a fundamental lack of empathy with peoples whose beliefs are foreign to our own way of thinking.

In spite of the fact that conflicts between peoples have existed for so long, we have good cause to hope to remedy or mitigate this disturbing situation. I firmly believe that the multicultural World Wide Web facilitates the long-sought, far-reaching dialogue that will lead us to a solution.

Yet the road is fraught with complexities that promise challenges at every turn. We know that many of the modern inventions that enhance our civilization also pose risks to individual rights and freedom. The danger is that private information can be used to gain control over others. To others, privacy, perceived as secrecy and exclusiveness, is itself dangerously counter-productive to collective interests. As noted above, privacy must continuously be reevaluated, as we reinterpret the balance between the complexities of democracy and our common humanity. The real danger lies in embracing technological advances without developing corresponding ethical counterparts. Thus, our foremost unresolved challenge is represented in the inherent imbalance of the traditional science/humanities dichotomy that permits technological innovations to control our lives.

We've discussed how, in the Postmodern Era, no one theory can be the only correct one. The eminent point of view is outmoded. When we use the technical inventions of the Information Age, the world is open for all to learn and grow as human beings by accepting others as we want to be accepted by them. Being all-inclusive need not come at the exclusion of our own preferences, yet we must never forget that our freedom ends where it harms another human being.

Throughout the pages of *The Multicultural Challenge: A Visual-Cultural Guide to Coping in the Global Era*, education points to an answer. We must educate ourselves to understand the importance of inclusiveness, that each of us is but one among many.

At the end of the day, we need to tame our anxiety regarding future developments and changes in order to cope with realities in flux. We need to reexamine our actions and our relationships with everyone and everything. And finally, we need to ask ourselves, "How can I participate in and improve on the future of my fellow travelers?"

APPENDIX A
INFORMAL EXPERIMENTS

Deprivation of Sight

Sighted people tend to overlook some of the most significant ramifications of seeing, which include maintaining harmony and balance with our immediate surroundings. Experiencing sight deprivation can engender a greater appreciation for the role that spatial, kinesthetic, and tactile perceptions play in our interactions with our environment.

This experiment is designed to help you comprehend the difference between passive and active viewing. The experiment is unique in that you'll gain new awareness of the power of your other senses and how these senses, to some degree, can compensate for your loss of sight.

After you've completed the experiment, try to maintain the acuity of the additional perceptual skills you've explored and bring them to bear on your normal viewing experiences.

Instructions: With the assistance of a partner, walk blindfolded for at least fifteen minutes, using the guidelines below.

1. Begin by walking slowly around in your own room. Take notice of how you experience your body responding to moving in darkness. Talk about what you feel and think.
2. Start to touch and feel the different objects you encounter in the room. Talk about what you feel and think.
3. Continue the experiment outside; touch trees, leaves, and other objects in your natural surroundings. Talk about what you feel and think.
4. In order to internalize your discoveries, respond to the following questions in sequence:
    a. Are you able to identify objects without seeing them?
    b. How is this possible? Do you rely on other senses? Do you rely on previous experiences?
    c. How does the loss of vision affect your awareness of space?
    d. How does your awareness of sound help you orient yourself?
    e. How does visual deprivation affect your sense of kinetic balance?

f. Does your self-confidence change as the result of not being able to see?

g. Has your perception of time changed during the experiment?

h. To what extent do you find that your other perceptual faculties are compensating for your loss of sight?

i. To what extent are you relying on memories of previously experienced visual data?

j. Take off the blindfold. Now that you can see again, reconsider the role of visual observation in perception. Has the experience changed the dominance you previously assigned to visual perception?

Ten Modes of Perception

This exercise is designed to help you augment your visual awareness by training yourself to monitor and modify your perceptions. In technical terms, cognition makes acquired knowledge retrievable for reallocation in new space and time contexts, a process called *recontextualization.*

Instructions: Working alone or with a partner, choose a visual field for your object of study; it could be a work of art or a person. Using your selected field as an agent of information, verbally describe the information as you perceive it.

Next, refer to the table on page XX and identify the perceptual modes you used in your description—these will likely be the modes you tend to engage in automatically.

Now, return to your chosen visual field and try another description, this time applying each of the remaining perceptual modes that you didn't use initially.

Visual Memory

Most of us have the potential for eidetic recall, and using our visual memory on a regular basis will improve it. By exercising your visual memory you can experience greater ease in recalling perceptions, no matter which modality of seeing you use. Practicing visual memory recall also contributes to enhanced retention.

This experiment assumes your familiarity with each of the perceptual modes listed in the table on page XX—you'll work with these modes in the present experiment. The intent of the experiment is to make you aware of your visual memory and the accuracy with which you're able to recapture what you've seen. Use it as a platform for self-assessment.

Instructions: To benefit from the experiment, it's important to proceed step by step as outlined below. Do the following with a friend (we'll call him John) without giving him any forewarning.

Experiment I

1. Ask John to close his eyes and conjure up a mental picture of you.
2. Wait a minute before you ask John to describe what you look like.
3. Then ask John to open his eyes to check to see how accurate the description was.
4. Ask John to consciously study your visual appearance, taking in all visible detail.
5. Ask John to close his eyes for a second time and describe your appearance in greater detail, including color of eyes, hair, etc., and to continue with details of clothing.
6. When his description is complete, have John open his eyes to check for accuracy.

Experiment II

1. Choose a visual statement such as a photograph or a picture.

2. Ask another friend (this time let's call her Jane) to look at it with you. Again, don't give her the benefit of forewarning.
3. Remove the item. Pause for a moment, then give Jane a piece of paper and ask her to write a detailed description of what she has seen, while you write your own description.
4. Next, compare your written descriptions. Then compare your individual descriptions with the originally observed item. Notice how your own description is most likely vastly more detailed and accurate. Keep in mind that your friend did not have the same advantage as you, having had no prior expectation of the (written) verbalization process as an aid to memory recall of the visual statement.
5. Finally, assess the extent of this verbalization in enhancing the detail and accuracy of your description.

The Dollar Bill Speaks

This experiment demonstrates the cultural specificity of symbols. It also highlights the wealth of information, so often overlooked, found in everyday objects.

Instructions: From memory, draw the back of a US dollar bill. Now, take out a one-dollar bill and compare it to your drawing. Did you remember to include the treasury seal with the scales? How about the pyramid to the left of the central word *ONE*? Did you include the eye floating above the uncapped pyramid? How about the other details? Look at the dollar bill again:

1. You'll see two large circles on the bill. Within the circle on the left is a pyramid. Capping the pyramid is the all-seeing eye, an ancient symbol for divinity. A Latin inscription, ANNUIT COEPTIS, which means "God has favored our undertaking," is written above the pyramid. At the base of the pyramid is the Roman numeral for 1776. Another Latin inscription, NOVUS ORDO SECLORUM, which means "A new order has begun," is written below the pyramid.
2. Within the circle on the right is a bald eagle. The eagle was selected as a symbol for victory for two reasons: First, he's not afraid of a storm; he's strong, and he's smart enough to soar above it all. Second, he wears no material crown. The fledgling democratic republic had just broken from the King of England, and crowns were not in fashion. Also notice that the shield is unsupported. This country can now stand on its own. At the top of the shield you see a white bar signifying Congress, a unifying factor. The country was coming together as one nation. In the eagle's beak is an inscription, E PLURIBUS UNUM, meaning "One nation from many people."
3. Written in the center between the two circles is "ONE," and above it you can still find written, "IN GOD WE TRUST."

This is just one side of the dollar bill. The other side is equally rich in American symbolism. If you examine a bill from any other currency, the same holds true of that county's symbolism.

Tasting Cultures

In this experiment we visit local restaurants to explore some of the most rewarding cultural specificities available to us. But our interest in this exercise extends beyond the menu, to the entire dining experience. So let's go over a few pointers before we get into the methodology of this experiment.

Here a note of caution is in order: As you proceed, try to determine which aspects of the experience are authentic to the original culture, and which might have been modified to suit American tastes. For example, a sign written in Chinese in front of a restaurant in San Francisco that reads "Western Food, Hong Kong Style" presents an interesting reversal from the more commonly advertised "Chinese Food."

Once inside an establishment, you can learn a lot from observing other customers. Generally speaking, if most of the guests are of the same ethnicity as the owner of the restaurant, you can assume that the place at least approaches an authentic representation of that culture. Are guests there with members of their family? Also telling is how they relate to one another—the quality of voices, gestures, and general manners. Taking nourishment in a safe place has the effect of relieving our inhibitions. There's a good reason that business transactions are sealed over lunch; the ritual of "breaking bread" connotes the sharing of Earth's abundance on equal terms.

In addition to the customers, pay attention to the decorum of the staff. Note the food servers, their attire, the quality of the service, and who is served first—male, female, older, or younger guests. Observe the general architectural lay out: spatial arrangement, placement, and style of the furniture; general color scheme, decorative elements such as lighting, and of course the artwork; each element is chosen to enhance the intended atmosphere. Examine the menu; the size of the portion served; its visual presentation in terms of texture, color, and seasoning; and the quality and décor of tableware and cutlery—all serve as complementary elements that are essential to the experience.

(Finally, don't forget to leave a gratuity commensurate with culturally specific expectations.)

Instructions: Consider each restaurant visit in six steps and see what you can come up with:

1. Pick a partner who has a different cultural background from yours. Together, select a restaurant that strongly reflects one of your ethnicities.
2. Begin by analyzing the restaurant from your own perspective, identifying those features that seem normal or familiar to you, and then those that seem alien or strange. Use the above introduction as a guide to help you focus on details.
3. Since many food traditions are pancultural (soup served in bowls with spoons), while others are culture-specific (eating with fingers, sponge bread, chopsticks, or forks and knives), these similarities and differences contribute to the whole experience. Categorize your observations of any pancultural and culture-specific aspects that come to mind.
4. After recording your observations independently, compare notes with your partner. It's to be expected that you'll have different views—the differences are as important to acknowledge as the similarities.
5. Follow the same steps as above, this time at a restaurant corresponding with the other ethnicity.
6. To expand on this approach for learning about cultures, repeat the experiment with other partners of different cultures. Based on your observations of people, their physical characteristics, appearance, and clothing, try to extrapolate into these cultures' other areas of expression. Pay attention to your expectations in regard to the concept of constancy of similar differences; remain open to adjusting your initial assumptions when further data recommend it.

Exchanging Perspectives

Generally speaking, those of us who are morally convinced on any given issue seldom recognize their own intransigence. Moreover, strong objections to the views of others are often rooted in our own subconsciously held mental habits, steeped in culture-specific conditioning.

This exercise calls for the use of situational ethics, a basic tool necessary in functioning effectively in a pluralistic society. The purpose of this experiment is to help you experience the hard work involved in diffusing animosity, to examine opinions that deviate from your own, and to meet the other person halfway. The experiment should help you learn what it takes to navigate a difficult issue while either maintaining your own convictions, or modifying them as the evidence may suggest. Additionally, the exercise will develop your capacity to anticipate divergent points of view and accept that opposing arguments originate in convictions that are as deeply felt by others as yours are by you.

Most importantly, this exercise should help you gain mutual understanding and respect for people who are different from you, and help you answer questions that plague all of us in our weakest moments when regarding others: Why can't you be more like me? Why can't you think more like me? What's wrong with you, anyway?

Instructions: Together with a friend (preferably one from a different culture), choose a volatile subject, such as abortion or the death penalty, that you disagree on. (If you feel that this exercise could jeopardize a friendship, try a less affective version by examining the viewpoints of a controversial public figure, such as a politician or talk show host.)

1. As in a formal debate, begin by considering arguments that favor the problem, that is, the *pro* position. Then have your friend introduce the opposite side, the *con* position.

2. Each of you should then write down your arguments, going from the general to the specific. Your respective lists should address the following:

   a. factuality
   b. moral perspectives
   c. societal implications.
3. Reverse positions with your friend; invest an equal amount of time and effort in completing your respective list of arguments.
4. Support your arguments with relevant examples.
5. Compare your lists in the following ways:
   a. your pro list to your friend's con list
   b. your con list to your friend's pro list
   c. your pro list to your friend's pro list
   d. your con list to your friend's con list.

At this point, you should be ready to mediate between opposing views and find points of reconciliation that will satisfy both of you. How do your lists compare? When examining your friend's list in response to step 1, did you notice that your friend's position came from his or her own frame of reference?

You might want to repeat this experiment with someone of another gender, age, or profession.

What insights have you gained as a result of exploring viewpoints from multiple perspectives?

APPENDIX B
GUIDE TO THE FORMAL ELEMENTS

The formal elements, such as colors, lines, and shapes, also known as artistic means, comprise the artist's vocabulary, a language in its own right, with a grammar as varied as the spoken languages of the world. We analyze formal elements in order to explore the thoughts and feelings an artist expresses through his or her work. Here we look at art from the artists' point of view, since they are the ones who know the grammar and use the vocabulary of art making. (Appendix C addresses art from the viewer's point of view.) We'll come to appreciate artists' ability to unlock the potentials and negotiate the limitations of the elements they choose in the risky give-and-take of communication. The formal elements represent endless possibilities on a palette.

An artist won't likely employ the entire catalogue of formal elements in one rendering, nor will he or she place the same emphasis on any one of them. Some artists like to explore the expressivity of line, for example, while others focus on color. Culture, era, school, and style all predicate how artists use their respective vocabularies. The priority of any of the artistic means will vary from culture to culture, era to era, and artwork to artwork.

Traditionally, an artist would have a prescribed mental image of what he or she was about to create, but this is no longer the case; many contemporary artists use the very act of painting as their inspiration, so the creative process itself becomes a major factor in determining the expression.

Frequently an artist makes a rough sketch of the general layout of the work. This is done in order to capture the composition of the work as a whole. The composition refers to the structure of a work in terms of its spatial organization—the placement of the formal elements within the format of the painting. The composition defines the structure of the work in terms of its dynamics, balance, or intended lack thereof.

We should bear a few caveats in mind as we consider the formal elements:

1. Though the formal elements are universal, artists tend to employ them in culturally specific ways. Composition and space are aspects that all artists must address, but cultures traditionally assent to their own priorities and preferences of the other elements. Additionally, postmodern artists often employ formal elements with ironic intent.
2. It's not entirely realistic to discuss the formal elements in isolation from each other; there's a vital interplay between all of the elements, as their character changes according to the pictorial context in which they appear.
3. Additional considerations come into play when we examine the aesthetic appearance of the formal elements, such as those related to the media and the tools employed. For example, colors applied with a palette knife on a textured surface like wood create a very different experience from watercolors brushed on rice paper.
4. Finally, the list below is ordered alphabetically rather than hierarchically, and is by no means comprehensive.

Color

A color is a reflection of diffused light upon a surface. Artists employ colors for various purposes, from rendering optical reality to evoking specific feelings and moods in the viewers.

- The character of a color depends on the amount and type of pigmentation, which determines if the color is opaque or translucent.
- Each color can be identified in reference to hue (red, green, blue, etc.), saturation (intensity of color), and value (amount of darkness or lightness in a color).
- The spectrum of colors is divided into primary, secondary, and tertiary colors, each in reference to whether they occur in a pure (undiluted, unmixed) or mixed form.

- Colors that appear to approach, or to come forward, such as red, orange, and yellow, are referred to as warm. Colors that appear to recede, such as blue, purple, and green, are referred to as cool.
- Complementary pairs are colors that generate the strongest contrasts, such as red and green, blue and orange, or yellow and purple.
- A single color used in its various range of values, known as a monochromatic palette, gives the effect of pictorial unity. This quality of unity allows the artist greater freedom to crowd the pictorial space with content elements without appearing chaotic.
- Mixed colors vary from flat (a single hue over an area) to speckled. The degree of color mixing may either soften the image or create a harsher impression.

Colors have a range of both culture specific and psychological properties. White is the color of sorrow and death in much of Asia, while black is the color of mourning in the West. Artists and psychologists recognize the emotional properties of colors. Blue, for example, the color of the sky and the seas, universally evokes a sense of calm.

Form, Shape, Volume

Form can be used in an artwork in a realistic, descriptive fashion, and it can also be used abstractly. Form is defined by shape or volume. Any extended line that ends where it began constitutes a two-dimensional shape, a modification and elaboration of line. Shape is an enclosed two-dimensional area, separating it from its surroundings. When shape is modeled to give the impression of a three-dimensional form, we describe it as having volume.

Ancient and modern sculptures rely on the elements of volume, shape, and line. Three-dimensional art forms also give play to light and shade. Contemporary artists fully explore these formal elements in their multi- and mixed-media creations.

Light and Shade

Shade is the gradation of light applied to objects in order to create and define a three-dimensional form through the modification or elaboration of color. It can be used to indicate a source of light, and/or accentuate the volumetric or weight aspect of a mass. When used in contrast to light, shade can be a space-creating device, communicating an illusion of distance and depth that frees objects from their background.

- The presence of light, illuminating areas within the composition, is achieved by applying lighter colors to a given area in order to create an illusion of a light source, such as the sun or a lamp.
- The presence of shade is achieved by modeling with darker colors on selected objects, giving an illusion of a three-dimensional form.
- The symbolic function of combining light and shade creates an illusion of time of day or night, and/or of good or evil, particularly in religious paintings.

Line

A line is the track of a moving point covering the distance between two objects; it is inherently one-dimensional.

- Lines contour and define shapes and objects.
- Lines don’t actually exist in nature, but are an illusory device applied by the artist in order to isolate pictorial elements.
- The expressive quality of a line varies according to whether it’s straight or curved, thick or thin, continuous or spaced.
- Staccato lines can be used to create rhythm.
- Lines can also be used for ornamentation.
- Repeated short lines, hatched or crosshatched, can create value differential and the illusion of shading and dimensionality.
- Curved lines are used to describe organic forms and frequently confer the feeling of sensuality.
- Angular and straight lines confer the feeling of a mechanized world.

Calligraphy, an art form in itself, depends on the dynamic usage of the line, investing it, as it were, with life. This tradition continues to be upheld in Chinese and Islamic art.

Plane

A plane is a flat surface, an area between two points or objects. It is inherently two-dimensional. To the painter, the canvas or paper constitutes a confined physical plane onto which the artist projects a vision. Often an artist's first move is to assess the capacity of a given space (a canvas, wall, etc.) to determine if it is ideal for carrying out his or her planned work.

Perspective

Perspective is a primary space-creating device. Perspective refers to the various techniques used to either define a particular angle of vision or aspect of an object, or to specify relations between pictorial elements. Below is a list of commonly used perspective techniques.

- One-Point (also known as Euclidian or linear perspective): This perspective uses a linear or eye-level horizon line on which parallel lines meet at a vanishing point in the distance. The viewer observes as if from a stationary angle of vision, placed on the outside looking into a scene, which creates the illusion of deep space.
- Vertical: This is a ladder perspective in which content elements are placed one above the other, without changes in size or depth, maintaining an illusion of a two-dimensional, flat surface.
- Worm's-Eye: Everything is perceived as if seen from below.
- Bird's-Eye: Everything is perceived as if seen from above.
- Aerial: This is an atmospheric or color perspective, rendering objects in the distance in fuzzy outlines and blurred, soft colors, which gives the impression of distance and depth in a painting.

- Foreshortening: This technique uses direction of lines to indicate depth by creating an illusion of a three-dimensional space on a two-dimensional surface.
- Hierarchical: This technique renders the size of an object in relation to its emotional and symbolic importance without regard to its actual optical size; this is also referred to as a conceptual perspective. This perspective is often employed in religious art.
- Multiple: Occurs when the artist combines more than one perspective. This perspective is historically prevalent in the Far East and has regained favor among artists throughout the world.

Space

Spatial organization provides the general structure of the composition, dealing with balance and focal point(s) in reference to the distribution of content elements. Space can be occupied or void, also referred to as positive or negative space. Western art historians refer to void as negative space. In Eastern paintings, empty space, or space left unoccupied, is considered the primordial place from which all forms come. Traditionally, empty space is an invitation to meditate, as it allows the promise of additional forms to emerge.

Texture

Texture refers to an object's specific surface quality.

- Texture is achieved in various ways, realized either by manipulation and/or elaboration of line in visible, patterned strokes; and/or by color, using impasto techniques (for example, applying thick, heavy paint that may reveal brushstrokes, or by applying pigment in very thin, transparent layers).
- Texture defines the quality of any created surface; it can be rendered in all gradations of either smooth or rough, slick or grained, soft or hard, transparent or opaque.
- Depending on the degree of intended realism, texture can be so lifelike that it is referred to as having a tactile quality.

In general, varying textures give an artwork the illusion of the presence of its subjects. On the other hand, the typical smooth surfaces applied to volumetric figures in the art of India are used to convey sensuality and also invite tactile responses in viewers.

APPENDIX C
GUIDE TO ANALYZING A WORK OF ART

It's impossible to meet new experiences with completely objective, unconditioned eyes. Analyzing art breaks the mold of the unconscious perceptual habits we've developed all our lives, enhancing our ability to cope with unfamiliar or unexpected cultural aspects that modern technology brings us face-to-face with daily.

Art analysis combines an understanding of art-making techniques and an artwork's cultural context of time and place. Seeing—observation—ideally leads to interpretations based on a cognitive understanding of the visual or emic aspect (that is, the operative character of the formal elements), as well as the specific cultural context, or etic aspect. This process encourages us to ask questions, gather evidence, and suspend judgment until we've interpreted the evidence. What we take from a work of art is commensurate with the energy we invest in the interpretive effort.

Step 1. Simply meet with the artwork as you would a human being. The first encounter is always a very personal experience and is a matter of inner dialogue and invitation, spontaneously enjoying the aesthetic aspects of the work. Retain this first impression for later retrieval.

Step 2. Verbalize your visual perceptions by inventorying its content elements (aspects that make up the content or subject matter of a painting), describing the work of art as if over the phone. This step is an orientation and the beginning of a systematic analysis:

- Describe the component parts of the art work, starting from the general (the largest entity) to the specific (the smallest details).
- Identify any iconographic elements (presence of visual signs intended to carry symbolic meaning).
- Identify medium(s) and format (for example, size).
- Consider the work's condition of preservation.

Step 3. Investigate, examine, and analyze art as an independent nonverbal language—the emic aspect (see "Guide to the Formal Elements" in appendix B on page 136).

Step 4. Art tells us about the culture from which it originates. We identify components of the context by taking sociohistoric as well as culturally conditioned conventions into consideration, including the meaning of the iconography (iconology).

Step 5. Integrate the visual aspects with the contextual information, together with ideas from additional sources including professional interdisciplinary appraisals and interpretations.

Step 6. Each time you examine a work of art you're re-creating it. Both you and the artwork change over time. Consequently, your experience with it is also subject to change. Recall your first impression of the work. In what way has your probing changed your understanding and appreciation?

NOTES

Chapter 1: Processing Visual Perceptions

1. Impressionism, an art movement that originated in France, was first exhibited in 1874. Artists working outdoors began to experiment with the so-called spectrum palette, relying on optical mixing to capture the impression of light on color and colors' various responses to light at different times of day. Two important exponents are Claude Monet and George Seurat. Op art, also known as "retinal painting," was a popular art movement in the 1960s that explored optical illusions, perceptions, and their physical and psychological effects. Two important exponents are Richard Anuszkiewicz and Bridget Riley.
2. Mahony, *Artful Universe*, 75-76.
3. Interestingly enough, while tourists seem to be in a discovery mode, they often seek to confirm rather than truly discover. We see this in the way they take snapshots of famous sights with themselves included in the foreground of the image, as though proclaiming to the world, "I was there." Immigrants who live for extended periods outside of their country of origin, on the other hand, live in the discovery mode, as discussed in chapter 4.
4. Dimont, *Jews, God and History*.
5. Wittgenstein, *Tractatus Logico-Philosophicus*.

Chapter 2: Decoding Art

1. See Panofsky, *Study in Iconology*, 43. Following this book's publication art historians began to make a distinction between iconography, the visual aspect of a symbol, and iconology, the interpretation of the visual aspect, which Panofsky defined as the intrinsic meaning or content.
2. Modern technology affords yet another avenue for recontectualization. The Metropolitan Museum of Art, like so many other museums and galleries, has placed its collection on the Internet. Masterpieces from around the world can be accessed free of charge through the museum's *Timeline of Art History* located on the museum's Web site, www.metmuseum.org. The site provides excellent digital photos for

every art lover to study at leisure. The World Wide Web offers sites devoted to art from all times and places. Another outstanding example is a global art gallery called HimalayanArt.org, which compiles Tibetan art from private and public collections from all over the world, making it accessible for all to enjoy. Tibetan art, in accordance with its Buddhist essence, exists just as it has since its inception, outside of space and time, in a realm of virtual reality. The Web site exhibits the imagery with digital accuracy in a format that allows for increasing and decreasing the magnification of details. By clicking on a detail, the user can access the iconography, iconology, and other useful information. This Web site liberates Tibetan art from its isolation and places it firmly within our reach as part of our artistic world heritage.

3. Be aware that the historical approach is neither singular nor definitive, as there are as many variations of this perspective as there are critics. For an in-depth discussion of some of these variations, see Cahill, "Three Alternative Histories."
4. Danow, *Thought of Michail Bakhtin*, 142.
5. Andres Serrano, an American photographer of Afro-Cuban decent, provoked a public stir in 1989 with a photograph titled *Piss Christ.* First shown at the Cathedral Church of St. John the Divine in New York City, the red-tinged photograph portrayed a crucifix, submerged in a glass container of the artist's own urine. The work was received with heated debate, especially with the news that Serrano had received a grant from the National Endowment for the Arts. Artists cited free expression as the cornerstone for their creativity, while enraged conservatives called for censure in the name of ethics. The controversy, which led to an ongoing discourse regarding governmental support versus censorship of art, remains unresolved.
6. See Sullivan, *Three Perfections.*
7. Strassberg, *"I Don't Want to Play."*
8. Lippard, *Mixed Blessings.*

Chapter 3: Decoding People

1. Condon and Saito. *Intercultural Encounters with Japan*, 7.

2. The question is, when is old, old? Western cultures are often less respectful of their elderly and tend to isolate them, depriving them of multigenerational interactions. Old age can be thoughtlessly associated with narrow-mindedness, limited options, and poor mental and physical health. An interesting shift is happening as the baby-boomers age and demand recognition of their individuality, rather than a categorization based on age discrimination—especially in first encounters.
3. Kasindorf, "L.A. Man Sues."
4. We see conformity to these standards in the hair-straightening of women of African ethnicity, and in eyelid surgery as part of a general makeover popular among Asian women.
5. Mothers who enter their daughters in beauty contests gain a competitive edge by promoting the sexualization of girls, dolling them up in thinly camouflaged sex appeal to make them look like women before their time. What's the motivation for these mothers? Are they star-dazed exhibitionists living vicariously through their daughters? The chance of gaining social stature, name recognition, and financial reward are all compelling reasons for the sentimental mother who started out with dreams and ambitions of her own.
6. Suzuki, *Japanese and the Japanese,* 146-147.

Chapter 4: Processing and Decoding Cultures

1. See Fletcher, *Situation Ethics.*
2. See the introduction of Mead, *Culture and Commitment.*
3. Concurrent with consumers' economic-based world view is the conservative desire to preserve the status quo, while simultaneously feeling threatened that their cultural heritage is being compromised. Responding to these concerns is one of the more notable programs initiated in 1972 by the United Nations Educational, Scientific and Cultural Organization (UNESCO). By adopting a treaty known as the World Heritage Convention, the world community was called upon to take initiative to identify, select, and support cultural and natural properties of "outstanding universal value." This program is presently active in 192 nations. However laudable, it should not go unnoticed

that this list, currently containing 851 sites worldwide, inadvertently encourages world tourism, one of the world's largest industries, with corresponding negative consequences for the preservation of these sites.

4. Cited in Winston, "On the Ethics," 15.
5. In his autobiography, published posthumously in 1791, Franklin outlined thirteen virtues necessary in attaining moral perfection; virtue #6 reads, "INDUSTRY. Lose no time; be always employ'd in something useful; cut off all unnecessary actions." Covey streamlined the attainment of moral perfection in his 1989 publication of *Seven Habits,* in which habit #3, "Put First Things First," outlines time management strategies for the chronically busy.
6. Tu-Wei-Ming, *Humanity and Self-Cultivation.*
7. This variation on the traditional extended family was highlighted in the Pacific Forum on Families International Conference on Divorce, Re-marriage, Stepfamilies & Blended Families, held November 2010 in Kuala Lumpur, Malaysia.
8. Lindsey, "A Farewell," 37.
9. Chang, *Food in Chinese Culture.*
10. Even in less-hurried restaurants, the American custom of taking home leftovers in "doggy bags" would provide pause for many Asians, who would consider such a practice uncouth.
11. The content of enculturation in Jungian terminology would be the "collective unconscious," a generative, collective agreement that, according to some scholars' interpretation, is universally held. Though a child imbibes a large body of traditionally held, unquestioned assumptions that dominate his or her opinions, motivations, and actions, I beg to differ from the Jungian interpretation of the hereditary and universal aspects of the collective unconscious. In reality, it's both simpler and more complex than Jung claimed. The universal aspect is not universal in reality, but refers to the shared consciousness imbedded in the people of a culture who have undergone the same enculturation process. I do agree however that the content of enculturation provides the interior landscape within which an ordinary person is entangled, until of course that individual reevaluates his or her positions during maturation or otherwise changing environments.
12. See Oberg, "Culture Shock."

13. This trend has manifested itself in and around Los Angeles in the creation of China Town, Little Taipei, Little Saigon, Little Tokyo, and Little Seoul. These enclaves have grown into self-contained communities that in terms of bookstores, grocery stores, restaurants, and other secular facilities re-create aspects of the respective cultures from their countries of origin. Particularly houses of worship, temples, and shrines, all of which were carefully constructed in traditional styles, serve to give a feeling of an authentic home to the diaspora. Most likely it is only in the hinterland of Asia that one still can find places resembling the above enclaves, since metropolitan Asia to a large extent is modernized. For visitors and locals these places present interesting glimpses of Asia, with their nostalgic imagery of a culture frozen in time.
14. Indian marriage proposals found in classified ads echo the ancient attitude of light-skinned people being superior to those with darker skin. Personal ads placed by light-skinned men seeking equally light-skinned women imply that these men would not compromise their perceived value inherent in the color of their skin. Even the occasional ad stating "not concerned" with the darkness of the woman's skin, or "skin color optional," suggests prejudice toward that particular quality.
15. Switzerland offers a different model and illustrates how convoluted immigration issues really are. Switzerland's citizenry is comprised of four ethnic groups: Germans, French, Italians, and the semi-official Romansh. The Swiss protect themselves from the influence of outsiders simply by employing an extremely strict immigration policy, making it virtually impossible to become a citizen of that country if you weren't born there.
16. "Multiculturalism," Ayn Rand Institute.
17. From national organizations like the RainbowPUSH Coalition (www.rainbowpush.org) to regional and local programs like the Mosaic Coalition (www.nycid.org), resources supporting multicultural education broaden awareness and sensitivity, especially in the younger generation. A further example is the Pennsylvania Psychological Association's Multicultural Resource Guide, available on its www.papsy.org Web site.
18. As portrayed by iconic American boosters like Benjamin Franklin and Horatio Alger, the liberty to reinvent oneself into the "self-made man"

is an enduring draw for enterprising individuals of any gender from around the globe. On the receiving end, Americans who expect newcomers to arrive completely cognizant of the social demands of this American brand of liberty themselves demonstrate a decided lack of cognizance.

19. Barber, *An Aristocracy of Everyone*, 4.

Chapter 5: Understanding Our Present and Creating Our Future

1. Steinhardt, "A Civil Liberties Ride on the Information Superhighway."
2. See Shah, "Causes of Poverty."
3. See Munroe, *Japanese Art After 1945.*
4. Vega, "Warning from Gore on Future."
5. The One Laptop per Child program addresses the digital divide problem for underprivileged children. MIT professor Nicholas Negroponte, in collaboration with experts from academia and industry, designed the XO laptop computer, built cheaply enough to distribute to children in developing nations. Negroponte's solution is a creative one: under the program, US consumers would also have access to XO laptops, although they'd be required to subsidize one for an indigent child for each unit purchased. See http://one.laptop.org.
6. See "What Makes a Cyber Criminal?" *BBC News*. E-mail scams frequently promise riches in return for a little help. The Nigerian oil tycoon who promises victims vast amounts of money if they will only supply him with their bank account number and perhaps send him enough cash for a plain ticket is a well known case in point. There are endless variations of these scams, and many have taken the bait. According to BBC News, Internet banking and credit card fraud is now the fastest growing sector of global organized crime, increasing at a rate of about 40 percent per year.
7. The Chinese government, having recognized computer addiction as a serious impediment to a productive lifestyle, has set up boot camps and clinics to provide self-discipline and professional treatment.
8. The sobering side of this reality is that the sites generating the most traffic on the World Wide Web are operated by purveyors of pornography. Apparently, some things never change.

9. To appreciate the new aesthetics that architects have already created or are in the process of creating the world over, see deputy-dog.com.
10. See www.projekt30.com.
11. California State University, *CSU Leader*.
12. Long Beach City College, *Schedule of Classes*, 139.
13. Shanahan, "Free 'Wiki' Textbooks."
14. See for example Manuel, *Popular Music,* v.
15. Quoted from a speech delivered by Bill Clinton at Yale University on October 31, 2003, at the invitation of the Yale Center for the Study of Globalization; see Clinton, "Security and Prosperity."
16. Flam, "Culture Express," 206.
17. Association for Asian Studies, *Asian Studies Newsletter,* 11.
18. An updated draft of the Universal Declaration of Human Rights is available at www.worldsreligionsafter911.com.
19. Buruma and Margalit, *Occidentalism*, 39.
20. Considering the EU's halting steps to find common ground and mutually beneficial goals for its members, it's remarkable that these historically hostile nations have created a common currency in addition to passports, opening their borders and allowing citizens within the EU to travel and work freely in the country of their choice. In spite of the economic successes, the lofty goal of drafting a common constitution has eluded the EU. Drafts on drafts have been discarded as national interests have come to the forefront and old animosities have flared up. The currently proposed constitution requires a reevaluation of national values and a consensus as to a new set of ethics, setting the common good above that of the nation-state.
21. Robinson et al., "Effects of Fast Food."
22. Zizek, "How China got Religion."
23. Nuridsany, *China Art Now*, 71.
24. Dadaism, a major art movement, was founded in Switzerland in 1916.
25. United Nations Educational, Scientific and Cultural Organization. *Recommendation Concerning the Status*.
26. Jameson, *Singular Modernity*.
27. See www.thehungersite.com.
28. Yunus and Jolis. *Banker to the Poor*, 2003.
29. In some New York City restaurants, customers requesting a glass of tap water are asked to pay extra, with proceeds going to the funding of

wells in developing countries. This creates awareness and a personal connection with those less fortunate. With wealth comes the social expectation and acceptance of *noblesse oblige*.

30. Despite privacy concerns, biometric scanning technologies are already available for consumer applications. In a recently reported news story, a customer in the checkout line at a supermarket, rather than pulling out his credit card, held up the palm of his hand and demanded the checker scan it. Upon repeated request for his credit card and repeatedly getting the same answer, the checker called the manager. The manager was also confused, but nonetheless complied and scanned the customer's palm, whereupon payment was authorized.
31. Paz, *The Bow and the Lyre*, 97, 117.
32. Peres, "Thoughts on Education."
33. See Goleman, *Emotional Intelligence;* Damasio, *Looking for Spinoza.*
34. The term "shock and awe" characterized the US military doctrine applied to a policy of preemptive warfare, implemented by the Bush 43 Administration in its 2003 invasion of Iraq.

Epilogue

1. The International Committee on Intellectual Cooperation was commissioned by the League of Nations in 1922 to further "intellectual work and international relationships between scientists, researchers, teachers, artists and members of intellectual professions…." Members serving with Einstein included Henri Bergson, Marie Curie, Béla Bartók, Thomas Mann, and Paul Valery. See League of Nations, "Intellectual Cooperation and International Bureaux Section, 1919-1946."
2. English translation from the original German by Ingrid Aall.

BIBLIOGRAPHY

by Chapter

Prologue

Patton, Michael Q. *Qualitative Research & Evaluation Methods.* 3rd ed. Thousand Oaks: Sage, 2002. Print.

Chapter 1: Processing Visual Perceptions

Crary, Jonathan. *Technique of the Observer: On Vision and Modernity in the Nineteenth Century.* Cambridge: MIT P, 1990. Print.

Dimont, Max I. *Jews, God and History.* 1901. New York: Signet, 1994. Print.

The Exorcist. Dir. William Friedkin. Perf. Ellen Burstyn, Max von Sydow, Lee J. Cobb, and Linda Blair. Warner Bros., 1973. Film.

Klimesch, Wolfgang. *The Structure of Long-Term Memory: A Connectivity Model of Semantic Processing.* Mahwah: Lawrence Erlbaum, 1994. Print.

Mahony, William K. *The Artful Universe: An Introduction to the Vedic Religious Imagination.* SUNY Series in Hindu Studies. Albany: State U of New York P, 1998. Print.

Sontag, Susan. *On Photography.* New York: Farrar Straus & Giroux, 1977. Print.

Wittgenstein, Ludwig. *Tractatus Logico-Philosophicus.* Trans. D.F. Pears and B.F. McGuinness. Milton Park: Routledge, 1962. Print.

Chapter 2: Decoding Art

Abell, Walter. *The Collective Dream in Art: A Psycho-Historical Theory of Culture Based on Relations between the Arts, Psychology, and the Social Sciences.* Cambridge: Schocken, 1957. Print.

Anderson, Richard L. *Calliope's Sisters: A Comparative Study of Philosophies of Art.* Upper Saddle River: Prentice Hall, 1990. Print.

Cahill, James. "Three Alternative Histories of Chinese Painting." *The Franklin D. Murphy Lectures IX.* Spencer Museum of Art. Lawrence: UP of Kansas, 1988. Print.

Cotter, Holland. "Eastern Art through Western Eyes." *The New York Times* 10 July 1994: H1+. Print.

Danow, David K. *The Thought of Michail Bakhtin: From Word to Culture.* New York: St. Martin's, 1991. Print.

Dimock, Edward C. "On the Translatability of Poetry." *The Sound of Silent Guns and Other Essays.* Oxford: Oxford UP, 1989. Print.

Ecker, Gisela. *Feminist Aesthetics.* Boston: Beacon, 1986. Print.

Ettinghausen, Richard, Oleg Grabar, and Marilyn Jenkins-Madina. *Islamic Art and Architecture 650-1250.* New Haven: Yale UP, 2002, 355, pl. 493. Print.

Lippard, Lucy. *Mixed Blessings: New Art in a Multicultural America.* New York: New, 2000. Print.

Panofsky, Erwin. *Gothic Architecture and Scholasticism: An Inquiry into the Analogy of the Arts, Philosophy, and Religion in the Middle Ages.* New York: Meridian, 1966. Print.

---. *Study in Iconology*. Oxford: Oxford UP, 1939. Print.

Strassberg, Richard E., ed. *"I Don't Want to Play Cards with Cézanne" and Other Works: Selections from the Chinese "New Wave" and "Avant-Garde" Art of the Eighties.* Pasadena: Pacific Art Museum, 1991. Print.

Sullivan, Michael. *The Three Perfections: Chinese Painting, Poetry and Calligraphy*. New York: George Braziller, 1999. Print.

Chapter 3: Decoding People

Blommaert, Jan, and Jef Verschueren, eds. *The Pragmatics of Intercultural and International Communication: Selected Papers of the International Pragmatics Conference, Antwerp, August 17-22, 1987, Vol. 3, and of the Ghent Symposium on Intercultural Communication.* Amsterdam/Philadelphia: John Benjamins, 1991. Print.

Condon, John C., and Mitsuko Saito. *Intercultural Encounters with Japan: Communication—Contact and Conflict.* Tokyo: Simul, 1980. Print.

Forrest Gump. Dir. Robert Zemeckis. Perf. Tom Hanks, Robin Wright Penn, and Gary Sinise. Paramount, 1994. Film.

Kasindorf, Martin. "L.A. Man Sues to Take Wife's Last Name." *USAToday.com*. USA Today, 11 Jan. 2007. Web. 17 July 2008.

Suzuki, Takao. *Japanese and the Japanese: Words in Culture*. Tokyo: Kodansha, 1978, 146-147. Print.

Tootsie. Dir. Sydney Pollack. Perf. Dustin Hoffman, Jessica Lange, and Teri Garr. Columbia, 1982. Film.

Chapter 4: Processing and Decoding Cultures

Asad, Muhammad. *The Message of the Qur'an*. Gibraltar: Dar Al-Andalus, 1980. Print.

Barber, Benjamin R. *An Aristocracy of Everyone: The Politics of Education and the Future of America*. New York: Ballantine, 1992, 4. Print.

Berlinski, Claire. *Menace in Europe: Why the Continent's Crisis is America's Too*. New York: Three Rivers, 2007. Print.

Blair, Sheila S., and Jonathan M. Bloom. "The Mirage of Islamic Art: Reflections on the Study of an Unwieldy Field." *The Art Bulletin* 85.1 (March 2003): 152-184. Print.

Borst, Arno. *The Ordering of Time: From Ancient Computus to the Modern Computer*. Trans. Andrew Winnard. Cambridge: Polity, 1993. Print.

Chang, K.C. *Food in Chinese Culture: Anthropological and Historical Perspectives*. New Haven: Yale UP, 1995. Print.

Covey, Stephen R. *The Seven Habits of Highly Effective People*. New York: Simon & Schuster, 1989. Print.

Eisler, Riane. *The Chalice and the Blade*. New York: HarperCollins, 1986. Print.

Fishman, Ted C. *China Inc.: How the Rise of the Next Superpower Challenges America and the World*. New York: Scribner, 2005. Print.

Fjordman. "Swedish Welfare State Collapses as Immigrants Wage War." *The Brussels Journal*. Society for the Advancement of Freedom in Europe. 28 Mar. 2006. Web. 18 Aug. 2008.

Fletcher, Joseph. *Situation Ethics.* Louisville: Westminster John Knox, 1997. Print.

Foster, Hal, ed. Discussions in Contemporary Culture. Vol. 1. Dia Art Foundation. Seattle: Bay, 1987. Print.

Franklin, Benjamin. *His Autobiography.* Vol. 1, pt. 1. The Harvard Classics. New York: P.F. Collier & Son, 1909-14. Print.

Lindsey, Brink. "A Farewell to Culture Wars." *National Review* 25 June 2007: 37+. Print.

Mead, Margaret. *Culture and Commitment.* London: The Bodley Head, 1970. Print.

"Multiculturalism: The New Racism." *Impact.* Ayn Rand Institute. Nov. 2002. Web. 24 May 2008.

Oberg, Kalvero. "Culture Shock." *Series in the Social Sciences Report No. A-329.* Indianapolis: Bobbs-Merrill, 1954. Print.

Pickthall, Mohammed Marmaduke. *The Meaning of the Glorious Koran.* New York: Mentor, 1953. Print.

Tu-Wei-Ming. Humanity and Self-Cultivation: Essence in Confucian Thought. Berkeley: Asian Humanities, 1979. Print.

Weiner, Myron. *The Global Migration Crises: Challenge to States and to Human Rights*. New York: HarperCollins, 1995. Print.

Winston, Kenneth. "On the Ethics of Exporting Ethics: The Right to Silence in Japan and the U.S." *Criminal Justice Ethics* 22.1 (2003): 3-20. Print.

Chapter 5: Understanding Our Present and Creating Our Future

Association for Asian Studies. *Asian Studies Newsletter.* 52.1 (Feb. 2007): 11. Print.

Buruma, Ian, and Avinashai Margalit. *Occidentalism: The West in the Eyes of Its Enemies.* New York: Penguin, 2004, 39. Print.

California State University. *CSU Leader* 5.33, 28 Sept. 2006. Print.

Clinton, William J. "Security and Prosperity in the 21st Century." *YaleGlobal Online.* Yale Center for the Study of Globalization. 31 Oct. 2003. Web. 8 June 2008.

Condry, Ian. *Hip Hop Japan: Rap and the Paths of Cultural Globalization Transnational Perspectives on Media and Culture.* Durham: Duke UP, 2006. Print.

Dalai Lama. *The Universe in a Single Atom: The Convergence of Science and Spirituality*. Morgan Road, 2005. Print.

Damasio, Antonio. *Looking for Spinoza: Joy, Sorrow, and the Feeling Brain*. New York: Harcourt, 2003. Print.

Dorf, Richard C. *Computers and Man.* 3rd ed. San Francisco: Boyd & Fraser, 1982. Print.

Flam, Jack D. "Culture Express: The Role of Museums." *ARTnews* May 1988. Print.

Goleman, Daniel. *Emotional Intelligence: Why It Can Matter More Than IQ*. New York: Bantam Dell, 1995. Print.

Hallengren, Anders, ed. *Nobel Laureates in Search of Identity and Integrity: Voices of Different Cultures*. New Jersey: World Scientific, 2005. Print.

Heelas, Paul. *Religion, Modernity and Postmodernity (Religion and Spirituality in the Modern World)*. Oxford: Blackwell, 1998. Print.

Herman, Andrew. *The World Wide Web and Contemporary Cultural Theory: Magic, Metaphor, Power*. New York: Routledge, 2000. Print.

Huehls, Mitchum. "Knowing What We Are Doing: Time, Form, and the Reading of Postmodernity." *Cultural Critique* 61 (2005): 55-86. Print.

Jameson, Fredric. *A Singular Modernity: Essay on the Ontology of the Present*. London: Verso, 2002. Print.

Jules-Rosette, Benetta. *The Messages of Tourist Art: An African Semiotic System in Comparative Perspective (Topics in Contemporary Semiotics)*. New York: Plenum, 1984. Print.

Korten, David C. *The Great Turning: From Empire to Earth Community*. San Francisco: Berrett-Koehler, 2006. Print.

---. *When Corporations Rule the World*. San Francisco: Berrett-Koehler, 2001. Print.

Kymlicka, Will. *Multicultural Citizenship: A Liberal Theory of Minority Rights*. Oxford: Oxford UP, 1996. Print.

Laszlo, Ervin. *Quantum Shift in the Global Brain: How the New Scientific Reality Can Change Us and Our World*. Rochester: Inner Traditions, 2008. Print.

Lippard, Lucy. *Mixed Blessings: New Art in a Multicultural America.* New York: New, 2000. Print.

---. *On the Beaten Track: Tourism, Art, and Place.* New York: New, 1999. Print.

Long Beach City College. *Schedule of Classes* Spring. Long Beach: Long Beach City College, 2007, 139.

Macpherson, C. B. *The Political Theory Of Possessive Individualism.* Oxford: Oxford UP, 1962. Print.

Manuel, Peter. *Popular Music of the Non-Western World.* New York: Oxford UP, 1988, v. Print.

Munroe, Alexandra. *Japanese Art After 1945: Scream Against the Sky.* New York: Harry N. Abrams, 1994. Print.

Nuridsany, Michel. *China Art Now.* Paris: Editions Flammarion, 2004, 71. Print.

Paz, Octavio. *The Bow and the Lyre.* Trans. Ruth Simms. Austin: U of Texas P, 1956, 97, 117. Print.

Peres, Shimon. "Thoughts on Education." Weblog comment. Haaretz.com. Haaretz, 19 Oct. 2007. Web. 22 June 2008.

Robinson, Thomas N., et al. "Effects of Fast Food Branding on Young Children's Taste Preferences." Archives of Pediatrics and Adolescent Medicine 161.8 (August 2007): 792-797. Print.

Shanahan, Mike. "Free 'Wiki' Textbooks Planned for Developing Nations." *SciDev.Net.* Science and Development Network, 1 Sept. 2006. Web. 24 June 2008.

Shah, Anup, ed. "Causes of Poverty." *Globalissues.org*. Globalissues.org. 7 Nov. 2010. Web. 24 Nov. 2010.

Steinhardt, Barry. "A Civil Liberties Ride on the Information Superhighway." *The National Newsletter of the ACLU* 380 (Spring/Summer 1994):1. Print.

United Nations Educational, Scientific and Cultural Organization. *Recommendation Concerning the Status of the Artist: Adopted by the General Conference at its Twenty-First Session, Belgrade, 27 October 1980. UNESDOC.* PDF file. 23 June 2008.

Vega, Cecilia M. "Warning from Gore on Future." *San Francisco Chronicle.* 5 June 2005: A17. Print.

"What Makes a Cyber Criminal?" *BBC News*. BBC. 19 May 2008. Web. June 23 2008.

Yunus, Muhammad, and Alan Jolis. *Banker to the Poor: Micro-Lending and the Battle Against World Poverty.* New York: PublicAffairs, 2003. Print.

Zeman, Adam. *Consciousness: A Users Guide.* New Haven: Yale UP, 2003. Print.

Zizek, Slavoj. "How China Got Religion." *The New York Times.* The New York Times, 11 Oct. 2007. Web. 23 June 2008.

Epilogue

Einstein, Albert. Letter to Anathon Aall. 19 November 1927. MS.

League of Nations. "Intellectual Cooperation and International Bureaux Section, 1919-1946." *League of Nations Secretariat, 1919-1946. UNOG Registry, Records and Archives Unit.* United Nations Office at Geneva Library. Web. 26 Sept. 2009.

BIBLIOGRAPHY

Abell, Walter. *The Collective Dream in Art: A Psycho-Historical Theory of Culture Based on Relations between the Arts, Psychology, and the Social Sciences*. Cambridge: Schocken, 1957. Print.

Anderson, Richard L. *Calliope's Sisters: A Comparative Study of Philosophies of Art*. Upper Saddle River: Prentice Hall, 1990. Print.

Asad, Muhammad. *The Message of the Qur'an*. Gibraltar: Dar Al-Andalus, 1980. Print.

Association for Asian Studies. *Asian Studies Newsletter*. 52.1 (Feb. 2007): 11. Print.

Barber, Benjamin R. *An Aristocracy of Everyone: The Politics of Education and the Future of America*. New York: Ballantine, 1992. Print.

Berlinski, Claire. *Menace in Europe: Why the Continent's Crisis is America's Too*. New York: Three Rivers, 2007. Print.

Blair, Sheila S., and Jonathan M. Bloom. "The Mirage of Islamic Art: Reflections on the Study of an Unwieldy Field." *The Art Bulletin* 85.1 (March 2003): 152-184. Print.

Blommaert, Jan, and Jef Verschueren, eds. *The Pragmatics of Intercultural and International Communication: Selected Papers of the International Pragmatics Conference, Antwerp, August 17-22, 1987, Vol. 3, and of the Ghent Symposium on Intercultural Communication*. Amsterdam/Philadelphia: John Benjamins, 1991. Print.

Borst, Arno. *The Ordering of Time: From Ancient Computus to the Modern Computer*. Trans. Andrew Winnard. Cambridge: Polity, 1993. Print.

Buruma, Ian, and Avinashai Margalit. *Occidentalism: The West in the Eyes of Its Enemies*. New York: Penguin, 2004. Print.

Cahill, James. "Three Alternative Histories of Chinese Painting." *The Franklin D. Murphy Lectures IX*. Spencer Museum of Art. Lawrence: UP of Kansas, 1988. Print.

California State University. *CSU Leader* 5.33, 28 Sept. 2006. Print.

Chang, K.C. *Food in Chinese Culture: Anthropological and Historical Perspectives*. New Haven: Yale UP, 1995. Print.

Clinton, William J. "Security and Prosperity in the 21st Century." *YaleGlobal Online*. Yale Center for the Study of Globalization. 31 Oct. 2003. Web. 8 June 2008.

Condon, John C., and Mitsuko Saito. *Intercultural Encounters with Japan: Communication—Contact and Conflict.* Tokyo: Simul, 1980. Print.

Condry, Ian. *Hip Hop Japan: Rap and the Paths of Cultural Globalization Transnational Perspectives on Media and Culture.* Durham: Duke UP, 2006. Print.

Cotter, Holland. "Eastern Art through Western Eyes." *The New York Times* 10 July 1994: H1+. Print.

Covey, Stephen R. *The Seven Habits of Highly Effective People.* New York: Simon & Schuster, 1989. Print.

Crary, Jonathan. *Technique of the Observer: On Vision and Modernity in the Nineteenth Century.* Cambridge: MIT P, 1990. Print.

Dalai Lama. *The Universe in a Single Atom: The Convergence of Science and Spirituality*. Morgan Road, 2005. Print.

Damasio, Antonio. *Looking for Spinoza: Joy, Sorrow, and the Feeling Brain*. New York: Harcourt, 2003. Print.

Danow, David K. *The Thought of Michail Bakhtin: From Word to Culture.* New York: St. Martin's, 1991. Print.

Dimock, Edward C. "On the Translatability of Poetry." *The Sound of Silent Guns and Other Essays.* Oxford: Oxford UP, 1989. Print.

Dimont, Max I. *Jews, God and History.* 1901. New York: Signet, 1994. Print.

Dorf, Richard C. *Computers and Man.* 3rd ed. San Francisco: Boyd & Fraser, 1982. Print.

Ecker, Gisela. *Feminist Aesthetics.* Boston: Beacon, 1986. Print.

Eisler, Riane. *The Chalice and the Blade.* New York: HarperCollins, 1986. Print.

Ettinghausen, Richard, Oleg Grabar, and Marilyn Jenkins-Madina. *Islamic Art and Architecture 650-1250.* New Haven: Yale UP, 2002, 355, pl. 493. Print.

The Exorcist. Dir. William Friedkin. Perf. Ellen Burstyn, Max von Sydow, Lee J. Cobb, and Linda Blair. Warner Bros., 1973. Film.

Fishman, Ted C. *China Inc.: How the Rise of the Next Superpower Challenges America and the World.* New York: Scribner, 2005. Print.

Fjordman. "Swedish Welfare State Collapses as Immigrants Wage War." *The Brussels Journal.* Society for the Advancement of Freedom in Europe. 28 Mar. 2006. Web. 18 Aug. 2008.

Flam, Jack D. "Culture Express: The Role of Museums." *ARTnews* May 1988. Print.

Fletcher, Joseph. *Situation Ethics.* Louisville: Westminster John Knox, 1997. Print.

Forrest Gump. Dir. Robert Zemeckis. Perf. Tom Hanks, Robin Wright Penn, and Gary Sinise. Paramount, 1994. Film.

Foster, Hal, ed. Discussions in Contemporary Culture. Vol. 1. Dia Art Foundation. Seattle: Bay, 1987. Print.

Franklin, Benjamin. *His Autobiography.* Vol. 1, pt. 1. The Harvard Classics. New York: P.F. Collier & Son, 1909-14. Print.

Goleman, Daniel. *Emotional Intelligence: Why It Can Matter More Than IQ*. New York: Bantam Dell, 1995. Print.

Hallengren, Anders, ed. *Nobel Laureates in Search of Identity and Integrity: Voices of Different Cultures.* New Jersey: World Scientific, 2005. Print.

Heelas, Paul. *Religion, Modernity and Postmodernity (Religion and Spirituality in the Modern World).* Oxford: Blackwell, 1998. Print.

Herman, Andrew. *The World Wide Web and Contemporary Cultural Theory: Magic, Metaphor, Power.* New York: Routledge, 2000. Print.

Huehls, Mitchum. "Knowing What We Are Doing: Time, Form, and the Reading of Postmodernity." *Cultural Critique* 61 (2005): 55-86. Print.

Iriye, Akira. *Global Community: The Role of International Organizations in the Making of the Contemporary World.* Berkeley: U of California P, 2002. Print.

Jameson, Fredric. *A Singular Modernity: Essay on the Ontology of the Present*. London: Verso, 2002. Print.

Jules-Rosette, Benetta. *The Messages of Tourist Art: An African Semiotic System in Comparative Perspective (Topics in Contemporary Semiotics).* New York: Plenum, 1984. Print.

Kasindorf, Martin. "L.A. Man Sues to Take Wife's Last Name." *USAToday.com.* USA Today, 11 Jan. 2007. Web. 17 July 2008.

Klimesch, Wolfgang. *The Structure of Long-Term Memory: A Connectivity Model of Semantic Processing.* Mahwah: Lawrence Erlbaum, 1994. Print.

Korten, David C. *The Great Turning: From Empire to Earth Community.* San Francisco: Berrett-Koehler, 2006. Print.

---. *When Corporations Rule the World.* San Francisco: Berrett-Koehler, 2001. Print.

Kymlicka, Will. *Multicultural Citizenship: A Liberal Theory of Minority Rights.* Oxford: Oxford UP, 1996. Print.

Laszlo, Ervin. *Quantum Shift in the Global Brain: How the New Scientific Reality Can Change Us and Our World.* Rochester: Inner Traditions, 2008. Print.

League of Nations. "Intellectual Cooperation and International Bureaux Section, 1919-1946." *League of Nations Secretariat, 1919-1946. UNOG Registry, Records and Archives Unit.* United Nations Office at Geneva Library. Web. 26 Sept. 2009.

Lindsey, Brink. "A Farewell to Culture Wars." *National Review* 25 June 2007: 37+. Print.

Lippard, Lucy. *Mixed Blessings: New Art in a Multicultural America.* New York: New, 2000. Print.

---. *On the Beaten Track: Tourism, Art, and Place.* New York: New, 1999. Print.

Long Beach City College. *Schedule of Classes* Spring. Long Beach: Long Beach City College, 2007. Print.

Macpherson, C. B. *The Political Theory Of Possessive Individualism.* Oxford: Oxford UP, 1962. Print.

Mahony, William K. *The Artful Universe: An Introduction to the Vedic Religious Imagination.* SUNY Series in Hindu Studies. Albany: State U of New York P, 1998. Print.

Manuel, Peter. *Popular Music of the Non-Western World.* New York: Oxford UP, 1988. Print.

Mead, Margaret. *Culture and Commitment.* London: The Bodley Head, 1970. Print.

"Multiculturalism: The New Racism." *Impact.* Ayn Rand Institute. Nov. 2002. Web. 24 May 2008.

Munroe, Alexandra. *Japanese Art After 1945: Scream Against the Sky.* New York: Harry N. Abrams, 1994. Print.

Nuridsany, Michel. *China Art Now.* Paris: Editions Flammarion, 2004. Print.

Oberg, Kalvero. "Culture Shock." *Series in the Social Sciences Report No. A-329*. Indianapolis: Bobbs-Merrill, 1954. Print.

Panofsky, Erwin. *Gothic Architecture and Scholasticism: An Inquiry into the Analogy of the Arts, Philosophy, and Religion in the Middle Ages*. New York: Meridian, 1966. Print.

---. *Study in Iconology*. Oxford: Oxford UP, 1939. Print.

Patton, Michael Q. *Qualitative Research & Evaluation Methods*. 3rd ed. Thousand Oaks: Sage, 2002. Print.

Paz, Octavio. *The Bow and the Lyre*. Trans. Ruth Simms. Austin: U of Texas P, 1956. Print.

Peres, Shimon. "Thoughts on Education." Weblog comment. Haaretz.com. Haaretz, 19 Oct. 2007. Web. 22 June 2008.

Pickthall, Mohammed Marmaduke. *The Meaning of the Glorious Koran*. New York: Mentor, 1953. Print.

Robinson, Thomas N., et al. "Effects of Fast Food Branding on Young Children's Taste Preferences." Archives of Pediatrics and Adolescent Medicine 161.8 (August 2007): 792-797. Print.

Shanahan, Mike. "Free 'Wiki' Textbooks Planned for Developing Nations." *SciDev.Net*. Science and Development Network, 1 Sept. 2006. Web. 24 June 2008.

Shah, Anup, ed. "Causes of Poverty." *Globalissues.org*. Globalissues.org. 7 Nov. 2010. Web. 24 Nov. 2010.

Sontag, Susan. *On Photography*. New York: Farrar Straus & Giroux, 1977. Print.

Steinhardt, Barry. "A Civil Liberties Ride on the Information Superhighway." *The National Newsletter of the ACLU* 380 (Spring/Summer 1994):1. Print.

Strassberg, Richard E., ed. *"I Don't Want to Play Cards with Cézanne" and Other Works: Selections from the Chinese "New Wave" and "Avant-Garde" Art of the Eighties*. Pasadena: Pacific Art Museum, 1991. Print.

Sullivan, Michael. *The Three Perfections: Chinese Painting, Poetry and Calligraphy*. New York: George Braziller, 1999. Print.

Suzuki, Takao. *Japanese and the Japanese: Words in Culture*. Tokyo: Kodansha, 1978. Print.

Tootsie. Dir. Sydney Pollack. Perf. Dustin Hoffman, Jessica Lange, and Teri Garr. Columbia, 1982. Film.

Tu-Wei-Ming. *Humanity and Self-Cultivation: Essence in Confucian Thought.* Berkeley: Asian Humanities, 1979. Print.

United Nations Educational, Scientific and Cultural Organization. *Recommendation Concerning the Status of the Artist: Adopted by the General Conference at its Twenty-First Session, Belgrade, 27 October 1980. UNESDOC.* PDF file. 23 June 2008.

Vega, Cecilia M. "Warning from Gore on Future." *San Francisco Chronicle.* 5 June 2005: A17. Print.

Weiner, Myron. *The Global Migration Crises: Challenge to States and to Human Rights*. New York: HarperCollins, 1995. Print.

"What Makes a Cyber Criminal?" *BBC News*. BBC. 19 May 2008. Web. June 23 2008.

Winston, Kenneth. "On the Ethics of Exporting Ethics: The Right to Silence in Japan and the U.S." *Criminal Justice Ethics* 22.1 (2003): 3-20. Print.

Wittgenstein, Ludwig. *Tractatus Logico-Philosophicus.* Trans. D.F. Pears and B.F. McGuinness. Milton Park: Routledge, 1962. Print.

Yunus, Muhammad, and Alan Jolis. *Banker to the Poor: Micro-Lending and the Battle Against World Poverty.* New York: PublicAffairs, 2003. Print.

Zeman, Adam. *Consciousness: A Users Guide*. New Haven: Yale UP, 2003. Print.

Zizek, Slavoj. "How China Got Religion." *The New York Times*. The New York Times, 11 Oct. 2007. Web. 23 June 2008.

INDEX

Ingrid Aall is Professor Emerita at California State University, Long Beach (CSULB), where she taught History of Art and History of Culture/Religion in the Department of Art and the Department of Asian and Asian-American Studies. In addition to developing a General Education course in Cross Cultural Visual Literacy, she has conducted seminars on Problems of Contemporary Indian and Chinese Painting, Global Perspectives in Contemporary Popular Art, and Methodology.

Dr. Aall trained as an artist at the Oslo National Academy of Art, received a BA in Psychology and Aesthetics from the University of Oslo, an MA in Philosophy from the University of Oxford, and a PhD in History of Culture from the University of Chicago. She has presented papers and given lectures at universities in Bangladesh, Brazil, Canada, China, England, Iran, Ireland, Israel, Mexico, Norway, Russia, Thailand, and the United States.

Currently residing in California, Dr. Aall continues to travel and lecture in the United States and abroad.

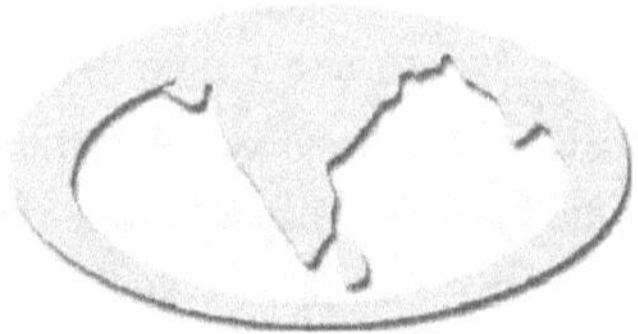

SASA Books is a project of the South Asian Studies Association, a recognized 501(c)3 non-profit public benefit corporation of scholars and others interested in South Asia. The corporation was organized in 2007:

a. To provide a public forum for research and scholarship on South Asia by means of an annual conference for the presentation of scholarly papers, lectures, panel discussions and other educational events.
b. To promote education about South Asia through such other programs, events and publications as may become feasible for the corporation to undertake.

SASA Books uses different model than trade publishers. Many services normally performed by the publisher are assumed by the author, allowing us to publish high quality, fully vetted materials at competitive prices. The SASA website is located at http://www.sasia.org. The email address is SASApubs@sasia.org.

www.ingramcontent.com/pod-product-compliance
Lightning Source LLC
LaVergne TN
LVHW050635100826
845148LV00011B/1878